Praise for *Forgiving Your Family*

There is nothing easy about forgiveness. It is messy work that is often done in small increments, but forgiveness holds the power for personal peace and healing. *Forgiving Your Family* will help people on this difficult but rewarding journey through powerful stories, practical applications, and scriptural inspiration.

—TERRY D. HARGRAVE, PhD
Professor of Counseling, West Texas A&M University
Author of *Families and Forgiveness: Healing Wounds in the Intergenerational Family*

Forgiving Your Family

A Journey to Healing

Kathleen Fischer

UPPER ROOM BOOKS®
NASHVILLE

The Upper Room® Web site: www.upperroom.org

Upper Room®, Upper Room Books®, and design logos are trademarks owned by The Upper Room®, Nashville, Tennessee. All rights reserved.

Scripture quotations are from the New Revised Standard Version Bible, copyright 1989 by the Division of Christian Education of the National Council of the Churches of Christ in the U.S.A. All rights reserved.

Cover design: Christa Schoenbrodt / studiohaus
Cover photo: Thinkstock
Interior design: PerfecType, Nashville, Tennessee
First printing: 2005

Library of Congress Cataloging-in-Publication Data
Fischer, Kathleen R. 1940–
    Forgiving your family : a journey to healing / Kathleen Fischer.
        p. cm.
    Includes bibliographical references.
    ISBN 0-8358-9802-4
    1. Forgiveness—Religious aspects—Christianity. 2. Reconciliation—Religious aspects—Christianity. I. Title.
    BV4647.F55.F57 2005
    248.4—dc22
                                                2004025994
Printed in the United States of America

For my family

Contents

Introduction

If the topic of family forgiveness comes up, what emotions does it stir in you? Do you think it means you must get back together with your sister who has hurt you deeply? Does it make you feel grateful that you found ways to reconcile with your mother before she died? Perhaps your father abused you when you were a child, and you don't see how you could possibly forgive him or how doing so would even help. Maybe you think forgiving means letting your mother-in-law get away with what she does to you. You may still be so furious at a former spouse that you don't even want to hear his name. Perhaps talk of forgiveness surfaces guilt about your inability to forgive your daughter when the gospel says you should forgive. If any of these statements sound like your thoughts, you are right in the thick of the normal, struggling human family.

Forgiving is one of the hardest tasks families face. Because the family is where we most count on being loved and accepted, it is also the context where we are hurt most deeply and often. Left unhealed, these wounds can destroy our health and happiness. Forgiving is as daily a part of family life as making meals and paying the bills.

Family members are the people with whom we have the longest and deepest ties. They remain crucial to us from birth to death as purveyors of the love, or lack of love, that so deeply shapes our identity. They see our best and worst qualities and respond with care and criticism. Holidays like Thanksgiving and Christmas, and special occasions like weddings and anniversaries, remind us that a house of love can also be a house of pain. We plan celebrations in the hopes that they will be enjoyable and satisfying. But family behavior is far from flawless. Spouses quarrel; siblings refuse to attend; cousins hold up the show; grandparents criticize. All of a family's hidden hostilities and irritating traits put in an appearance. Yet, year after year, most families try again. Even though we experience hurt and inflict it on others, we are also resilient.

Why is forgiving one another so hard for family members? And what makes forgiveness possible? This book seeks to answer those questions.

The initial chapters explain forgiveness and offer reasons for attempting it. Subsequent sections treat crucial aspects of forgiveness such as handling the desire for revenge, dealing with anger, letting go of grievances, and protecting ourselves from further harm. Throughout you will find emphasis on the difference small actions can make. Small actions prove especially important when forgiving seems impossible. A concluding chapter provides ideas for creating a family atmosphere in which forgiveness can more readily flourish.

Psychological research and resources ground the entire book. But while these remain indispensable to the work of forgiveness, they are not sufficient. Lasting forgiveness is a grace that rests finally on faith and prayer. Forgiveness is pivotal to Jesus' vision. He shows us that God meets us in human love and is with us in our efforts to heal relationships. Jesus gave his life to bringing about the kind of relationships we long to experience in our families. When we feel tempted to flee their demands, the gospel reminds us that redemption happens right here in the give-and-take of ordinary family life.

Families come in all shapes and sizes. They can be as small as two people or as large as ten and encompass one generation or several. Further differences result from divorce, adoption, personal choice, and diverse cultural norms. We usually define family as those with whom we have blood ties, but sometimes our family seems more truly comprised of friends who take the place of family.

What I say about forgiveness applies to all these kinds of families. I have created stories based on years of listening to clients, friends, and my own family members grapple with family relationships. Although my examples reflect no one's story in particular, they typify family struggle and victory. They embody what I have learned about roadblocks to forgiveness and breakthroughs to reconciliation.

Since forgiveness requires hard work, you may want a companion to journey with you through this book. For smaller matters the companion might be a friend, but for more serious hurts you may need a professional counselor. May this book lead you through pain, impasse, and fear into healing and peace.

Chapter 1

What Is Forgiveness?

J ohn is a gentle man in his late forties. But his typically
kind expression tightens as he talks about his struggle
to be civil to his stepson, Peter. Now a young adult, Peter
lives a good distance away from John, and they see each
other only a few times a year. Yet John can barely stand to
be around Peter, and this fact robs him of inner peace. He
should be able to get over what is bothering him, he tells
himself. "I've got to get to the point of forgiving him,
that's all. But only my mind can go there. My emotions
just can't."

John finds himself dreading each family gathering. He avoids Peter whenever possible and has been curt and cool when they are forced together. What he can't forgive, John says, is the way Peter has treated him over the years: trying to convince his mother not to marry John, refusing ever to accept him or open even slightly to him, and several times asking for money and then using it for drugs. How can John let go of all this and try again?

When the gospel ideal of forgiveness seems unreachable, as it does for John, a good starting place is to get clear about what forgiveness is and is not. When we forgive, what exactly are we doing?

> *Forgiving starts with choosing to let go of negative feelings, thoughts, and behaviors.*

Consider your own attempts at forgiveness. You may notice that the first turning point comes as you become able to release the anger and resentment that flared up when you were hurt and then took up residence in you. Forgiving starts with choosing to let go of negative feelings, thoughts, and behaviors. You refuse to use the offense as a weapon or an excuse for your own bad behavior.

Though a difficult and essential move, this letting go is only the first step. As forgiveness unfolds over time, our thoughts and feelings toward those who injured us become not only less negative but more positive. Though the offender may not deserve compassion, love, and generosity, gradually we become able to offer these qualities as gifts.

In forgiveness we make a U-turn in our thoughts, feelings, and actions. We experience the change of heart Jesus counsels. Forgiving is both a choice—actually many choices—and a continual acceptance of grace. Ultimately, for Christians, it rests on the realization that we ourselves have been graciously forgiven for all the ways we have hurt others. We are more like than different from those who injure us. Extending mercy to others is possible because we so often stand in need of it ourselves.

The forgiveness journey is frequently halting and imperfect. And each person's journey differs, depending on the closeness of a relationship, the seriousness of the injury, and the remorse or lack of it in the offender. Yet the various kinds of forgiveness share three fundamental elements: dealing with emotions, changing perspective on the person who inflicted pain, and opening ourselves to the possibility of reconciliation.

DEALING WITH ANGER AND OTHER EMOTIONS

Suppose your mother fails to attend your son's graduation and offers no good reason for not coming. You are mad and sad—not just for yourself but for your son, who had counted on his grandmother being there for his big day. So graduation is not what you thought it would be; you had pictured the family all together for a happy occasion. And your anger and sadness do not go away. They rise every time you think about it. In fact, you develop a stomachache whenever you tell others what your mother did. If you could put your feelings into words, they might sound like this: "OK, if your golf tournament means more to you than I do, don't expect me to come running the next time you need to see a doctor!"

An essential aspect of forgiving is learning how to lower the emotional volume inside us by processing feelings like anger. We're tempted to skip this step, hoping that feelings will just go away. But when emotions are strong, we usually cannot shake them off the way a dog sheds water after coming out of a lake. We need to find constructive outlets for the physical energy that often accompanies strong emotions, and we must change the grievance accounts that keep them stirred up. We may have to do this again and again until the negative emotion subsides.

Parents guide children's development in this aspect of forgiveness by helping them understand and manage their emotions. For example, as they look together at pictures in books, parents can ask children questions that teach them to notice their own and others' feelings: "His friend took his toy without asking. How do you think he feels? How would you feel if that happened to you? What else can he do when he is angry?"

Dealing with the emotion generated by a hurt rests on an honest acknowledgment of the truth about what has happened. We may be in the habit of saying, "That's OK," or "No problem," while seething inside. But forgiveness does not mean we must ignore the pain and pretend a hurt never happened. Neither does it mean condoning or trying to minimize what someone did.

The problem with forms of pseudoforgiveness like condoning or excusing is that they don't work for long.

The pain may go into hiding. But since it has never really been dealt with, it eventually festers again, like a wound that has not been properly treated. Suppose your dad forgets your birthday. You feel hurt, but you tell yourself that it is no big deal. Then his birthday comes, and you find yourself not wanting to send him a card.

Another crucial part of the emotional work of forgiveness is the refusal to get even. Our immediate instinct is to return hurt for hurt. Revenge promises to make us feel better, but it actually takes us down the road of unhappiness. Forgiving allows us to redirect our energies in positive ways. We become clear about what we want in a relationship and work toward that. Peace comes from living in the present, not backward toward the hurt or forward toward retribution. Awareness of the present moment heightens gratitude for what is beautiful and good about life in spite of this hurt.

Usually we have to choose to forgive before we feel like forgiving. We decide to forgive because it is a good thing to do, but at this point we do not feel much love for the person who hurt us. Gradually, as we work with the anger and pain, understanding and compassion grow.

CHANGING PERSPECTIVE ON THE ONE WHO HURT US

To forgive, we must change the way we view the person who hurt us. Usually we cannot make this shift in the first heat of emotion. When a family member offends us, thoughts and feelings reserved for an enemy replace the love we have felt for that person. Instead of the husband whose kindness, humor, and industry led us to marry him, we see only someone thoughtless, dishonest, and lazy. We embellish this negative image by recalling his previous offenses and irritating behaviors. Like a vacuum cleaner, we suck up any other grievances we can find. To forgive is to reframe your negative picture of a person, letting in awareness of his or her virtues, feelings, and beliefs. This new frame makes release and empathy possible. More positive emotions and attitudes gradually replace the negative.

Finding a new lens for seeing wrongdoers is a critical part of forgiveness.

In *Seasons of a Family's Life*, theologian Wendy M. Wright aptly describes this experience. At the end of a long, frustrating day, she finds herself standing with her arms crossed, staring angrily at her eleven-year-old daughter, who is acting snippy and being uncooperative. This attitude pushes Wright over the edge, turning daughter and mother into "enemies." Wright says that in that moment, eleven years of similar rude and rebellious moments fill her consciousness. She completely defines her daughter by these recollections. Mother and daughter exchange wounding words. Then, as tempers cool, there are grudging apologies. As the anger recedes further, Wright is able to let in all the good parts of her daughter and their relationship: loving exchanges, good times, affection given and received. By the next morning, genuine sorrow and reconciliation take place. Wright and her daughter can now talk about the whole experience.[1]

Finding a new lens for seeing wrongdoers is a critical part of forgiveness. We often realize that they are not totally bad persons but instead wounded, limited, struggling human beings like ourselves. This is the perspective Jesus shows when he loves the sinner and hates the sin, when he condemns the wrong but eats and drinks with the wrongdoer. He distinguishes persons from the hurts they inflict, looking with compassion on their personal history and current struggles.

> *While reconciliation is the hoped-for outcome of healing work, it does not necessarily follow from forgiving.*

Later we'll explore more fully the reality that some people have endured such horrible abuse from a family member that they should not try to see that person in a new light right now. What this would require is too painful or damaging or simply may be impossible. It is best for them to leave the judgment to God and get on with other aspects of their healing, such as stopping the effects of the abuse in their own lives.

OPENING OURSELVES TO RECONCILIATION

Reconciliation restores a relationship between family members. But it requires work by both parties. So while reconciliation is the hoped-for outcome of healing work, it does not necessarily follow from forgiving. Although people sometimes use the terms *forgiveness* and *reconciliation* interchangeably, important features distinguish these two realities.

First, forgiveness always precedes reconciliation. We don't truly get back together with family unless some level of forgiveness occurs. How can a relationship be restored if one person is still filled with rage or harbors a grudge, or the other is totally unrepentant? We may meet or talk to these persons again, but if the inner work of forgiveness has not happened, our hearts will still be closed against them.

Second, if forgiving and reconciling were identical, the person who hurt us could forever hijack our healing. In other words, we wouldn't be able to forgive until the offender was ready to restore the relationship. If he or she refused to apologize, we could not move forward with forgiving. This would put our healing in that person's power, allowing him or her to decide whether or not we recover from a hurt.

Reconciliation means mutual restoration. Forgiveness, on the other hand, is a decision made in an individual's heart. Of course, as forgiveness deepens, it becomes evident in outward expression toward the person who offended us. Nevertheless, we may forgive and, for various reasons, choose not to reconcile. The offender may remain unrepentant and disinterested in healing the relationship; getting back together may be neither prudent nor safe.

For our part, we need to remain open to the possibility of reconciliation should circumstances warrant it, particularly when the person who hurt us is a family member.

The very nature of family requires that we work at getting along with everyone. Staying open to reconciliation also readies us for grace when it arrives. One woman who suddenly felt herself free to reconnect with a niece after months of estrangement called this new freedom "an unrequested grace," so astonished was she by the breakthrough.

The gospel makes clear the centrality of reconciliation to the Christian life. John's Gospel offers us a vision of the new life that is possible for Jesus' followers. In the gospel ideal of community, individuals prosper insofar as they recognize their interrelationship with Jesus and everyone else. The image of the vine and the branches speaks to the bonds of family life.

> Just as the branch cannot bear fruit by itself unless it abides in the vine, neither can you unless you abide in me. I am the vine, you are the branches. Those who abide in me and I in them bear much fruit, because apart from me you can do nothing. (15:4-5)

No individual exists in isolation. As branches of an intertwining vine, our fruitfulness depends on abiding in community, the community grounded in God. Where possible, forgiveness should bear the fruit of reconciliation.

To sum up the key aspects of forgiveness, let's return to our opening story of John and his stepson, Peter. John has already begun the forgiveness journey, since he knows he needs to forgive and realizes that not doing so interferes with his own peace and family life. As he firms up the decision to forgive, what will it ask of him? First, naming and dealing with the emotions he feels—the hurt, anger, sadness, and fear that resulted from the ways Peter has hurt him. He will refuse to take opportunities to pay Peter back for that hurt, even by subtly giving him a cold shoulder at family gatherings.

John also needs to undertake the central work of changing his heart, beginning to reframe how he views Peter. When he starts to realize from Peter's perspective what it might be like to lose a father and then have another man move into his place, he can begin to understand the roots of Peter's behavior and move toward compassion for him.

Forgiveness does not demand that John keep shelling out money to Peter or that he accept Peter's rudeness as thanks. He can change his own actions, set limits, and insist on respect. Of course, if the two are to reconcile fully, Peter also has some work to do. He needs to walk in John's shoes for a while. But forgiveness from John's side has begun, paving the path to possible reconciliation.

Chapter 2

Why Should I Forgive?

A daughter stops blaming her mother for neglecting her as a child. A husband wrestles with rage after the revelation of his wife's affair. Two cousins meet for lunch to talk about their grievances with each other. As a counselor I watch countless family members struggle to forgive. Why are some consumed by rancor while others heal and move on? Among other factors, those who succeed in forgiving are moved by compelling reasons to do so. Let's look at those reasons so that we might find help, especially when forgiving is very difficult.

1. God forgives us. Willingness to forgive arises from the graced awareness that we ourselves need forgiveness. Examples of this recognition occur often in my own life. I may be angry with a family member for criticizing me, keeping secrets, or failing to pull equal weight on family projects. Then, to my chagrin, I catch myself doing the very same thing. The illusion that others are sinful and I am perfect bursts like a balloon, giving way to the realization that every one of us stands in need of mercy. No exceptions. God forgives us freely and repeatedly. Can we do any less for others? A biblical passage prods me when I withhold forgiveness:

> Forgive, and you will be forgiven; . . . for the measure you give will be the measure you get back. (Luke 6:37-38)

In the prayer Jesus taught his disciples, we find the following words:

> And forgive us our sins,
> for we ourselves forgive
> everyone indebted to us. (Luke 11:4)

How can we utter these words when we have hardened our hearts against those who have offended us? When we refuse to release wrongs, our prayers seem to bounce off God like tennis balls off a concrete wall. We suddenly know why Jesus said,

> Whenever you stand praying, forgive, if you have anything against anyone; so that your Father in heaven may also forgive you your trespasses. (Mark 11:25)

Recognizing forgiveness as God's free gift chips away at the barriers we erect to forgiving others.

Victor Hugo's *Les Misérables* tells the story of how one man, French prisoner Jean Valjean, is redeemed by the gift of forgiveness. Valjean, sentenced to a nineteen-year term of hard labor for stealing bread, gradually hardens into a tough convict. Upon his release from prison, Valjean wanders the village seeking a place to spend the night until a kind bishop offers him shelter.

That night Valjean waits until the bishop and his sister are asleep; then he steals the family silver. The next morning, policemen knock on the bishop's door, with the captured convict and stolen silver in tow. The bishop's response amazes Valjean and changes him for life: "Ah, there you are!" he says. "I am glad to see you. But I gave you the candlesticks also, which are silver like the rest, and would bring two hundred francs. Why did you not take them along with your plates?" Valjean stares at the bishop in disbelief. After the police release Valjean and leave, the bishop gives him the candlesticks, saying, "Forget not, never forget that you have promised me to use this silver to become an honest man."[1]

The bishop sets aside all thoughts of revenge, and his action moves Valjean to his very depths. He dedicates his life to helping others in need. Valjean's story shows that when we truly realize the meaning of being forgiven, we find salvation. *Les Misérables* is a parable of the way we are transformed by the God who is "merciful and gracious, slow to anger, and abounding in steadfast love and faithfulness" (Exod. 34:6). Our willingness to forgive rests on awareness of God's reconciling love.

2. The example of Jesus moves me. Jesus makes forgiveness pivotal to his teaching and models it from start to finish. He spends his entire life giving to others, but in the end he dies like a common thief. If ever someone had reason for resentment and revenge, Jesus did. Yet, even as he dies, he releases those who taunt, mock, and crucify him: "Father, forgive them; for they do not know what they are doing" (Luke 23:34).

Forgiveness characterizes not only Jesus' life and death but also his Easter appearances. Peter could not muster the courage to stand by Jesus in his loneliness and final anguish. Yet Jesus offers him several chances to heal his shame and express his love (John 21:15-19). Easter marks a fresh beginning and inaugurates a new age where forgiveness can freely flourish. Without forgiveness we would, like Peter, be forever bound by one action—an hour of weakness, an uncensored comment, a careless deed would forevermore define who we are. But the risen Jesus brings reconciliation, the release and restoration for which we yearn. He gives the Spirit along with the command to forgive. The spirit of Jesus makes forgiving possible.

3. This is not the kind of person I want to be. A woman comments on her refusal to forgive her husband: "It's not a part of myself I particularly like. But when I'm criticized and judged, I turn it around and do the same. When my trust is violated, I notice every bad quality in a person. I don't want to be like this anymore."

Each of us hopes to grow gradually into the virtues that characterize a Christian. Sometimes we notice that we are off course. Perhaps a close friend remarks about how much we harp on our mother's faults. Or a spouse complains that our unrelieved negativity is intolerable.

The recognition that we have strayed from the gospel path may also come to us in prayer. We see that dwelling on hurts keeps us from becoming the kind of person God wants us to be. As one woman acknowledged this truth, she said, "Now when I have certain thoughts, I don't let them in anymore. It's time to forgive."

We may also discover that we are attached to the role of victim. Like the prophet Jonah, angered by God's compassion for the city of Nineveh, we feel a little miffed when others repent. There are benefits to the victim status: Walking the moral high ground by virtue of being wronged. Seeing our own motives as pure. Inducing guilt and demanding apologies. Getting leverage in a relationship by bringing up past hurt. Even enjoying the sympathy of other family members. After returning from a retreat, a man declared: "I hate the way my refusal to forgive has twisted me into a permanent victim. I'm going to find a way to change it."

Not liking who we have become is one motive for forgiving. Another is witnessing family members locked in endless disputes, or grandparents filled with bitterness in their last decades. During my work in nursing homes, I was struck by how many younger family members vowed they would never turn into their older relatives. They could see firsthand how wizened and ugly people become after rehearsing others' wrongs for years. They wanted instead to imitate those older people who released their rancor and moved into the later years with grace and peace.

4. Holding this grudge is ruining my life. My clients describe a number of physical and emotional consequences of refusing to forgive. Like an acid, holding onto a hurt corrodes, gnawing away at health of mind and body. Some find it interferes with sleep. Anger wakes them up in the middle of the night, and they start ruminating on the wrong. Others report neck pain, headaches, and stomachaches. Studies show that chronic anger, blame, stress, and hostility take a toll on physical health. They negatively affect blood pressure, heart rate, and immune function.

Scientific research increasingly indicates that, in contrast, forgiving can lead to physical and emotional health. Neuroscientists have already shown that forgiving may decrease levels of stress hormones and improve sleep patterns. This, they suggest, may be just one of many links between forgiveness and healing. Other studies connect forgiving to improved functioning of cardiovascular and nervous systems. This translates into less stress, anxiety, and high blood pressure. It means more health, hope, confidence, and happiness.[2]

So we need to ask, is holding this grudge worth ruining my life? Sometimes releasing a hurt follows from awareness that the situation will not change, and we are making ourselves unhappy about it. Continuing to hold the grudge drains the energy we could give to other projects. We may spend most of our time obsessing about the situation and plotting revenge. Even children in a family can see that nursing a grudge makes a hurt last longer. Clearly this is not how God intends us to spend the gift of our brief life span. It may be time to let go, if only for our own sake.

5. *Not forgiving is destroying my family.* Families are like mobiles: touch any part of a mobile, and every other part moves. A sister's divorce and refusal to speak to her ex-husband affects all family members' relationship toward him. Can I still act friendly toward her former husband without my sister seeing me as disloyal? If I have a party, do I invite one and not the other, or must I have two parties to take care of the problem? When both show up at a wedding or funeral, the tension between the former couple mars the event for all who are aware of it.

Unresolved hurt affects the entire family system, including future generations.

Unresolved hurt affects the entire family system, including future generations. Knowing this, we may decide to work on forgiveness out of concern for the survival and health of our family. I remember when my brother and I had not spoken to each other for several months after a phone fight over my mother's care. I was walking with my husband on a park trail not far from our house. Suddenly three boys darted in front of us, laughing and tossing a softball to one another. The oldest boy looked just like my brother when he was about ten. Suddenly I glimpsed the way my mother must have seen him as her growing son, and I was nearly overwhelmed by an immense sadness. I realized how much our mother wanted us all to love one another. Family meant everything to her. Though I did not take immediate action, I knew a crack had opened in the wall I had erected against my brother.

Parents teach their children forgiveness above all by example. This modeling lodges more indelibly than anything else in children's minds. A mother reflects on this truth as she agonizes over the troubled behavior of her adult son: "I see now that what mattered was not only how I treated my son or how my husband treated him, but how we treated each other. I'd tell other parents that if they want their children to learn how to forgive, they should start with themselves." Concern for the moral development of children in our families is a powerful motive for practicing forgiveness.

6. *I care about these people, and we need one another.* Even happy families suffer and inflict pain. Forgiving family members can be hard because we expect more of them. But it can also be easier because these relationships are so irreplaceable and so central to our lives.

Pondering certain questions helps situate an offense within the history of the relationship:

- How does this hurt compare with what I love and value in this person or relationship?

- Is what happened worth being as upset as I am about it?

- In the bigger picture of my life and family relationships, is this situation worth all the energy I give it?

- What else is going on in my life that might account for how strongly I am holding on to this hurt? Am

I stressed and tired, feeling discouraged or upset about other matters?

• What will I gain by clinging to this wound? by letting go and moving on?

The most helpful practice is to take these questions to prayer, listening honestly to our deepest response. Such prayer situates an offense in the larger context of a relationship, preventing us from taking actions we will regret.

7. *I want this family pain to stop with my generation.* A couple comments: "We were given this garbage by our families and have suffered because of it. Wouldn't it be great if we could stop it right here and not pass it on to our children and their children?" Those who survive family violence sometimes experience great rage because they were powerless to prevent it. The power they have now, however, is to stop this legacy of abuse. "No more," they say. "My children are not going to endure what I did." But this means getting the toxins out of their own bodies and minds so that they do not poison the next generation.

I came to realize that my own family had a long habit of resolving hurts through cutoff—by shutting down relationships, stopping discussion, and dropping out of family groups. Neither my siblings nor I know exactly how this happened, but at some point we no longer had contact with the aunts, uncles, and cousins we once enjoyed. Fragmentary clues suggested reasons: Was my dad turned down when, in a desperate financial state during the Depression, he asked my uncle for a loan? Had an aunt criticized my mother's care for their mother? Like missing pieces in a jigsaw puzzle, incomplete information prevents us from making sense of the events. But we understood that the cutoff meant we no longer got to experience my aunt's homemade German noodles or July picnics around tables heaped with hot dogs and watermelon.

My family faces the challenge of stopping this pattern of using cutoff instead of forgiveness to handle family disputes. In similar ways, other families are motivated to deal with their own past pain when they see the impact of family patterns on succeeding generations.

8. *Life is too short.* When tragedy struck the United States on September 11, 2001, it instantly put life in perspective. In light of the sudden deaths of thousands of innocent people, many Americans realized that little grievances with family members were just not worth it. Deeply moved by final calls to loved ones made from cell phones in the burning Twin Towers or in hijacked airliners about to crash, we in turn wanted to call a husband, son, sister, or mother and say, "I love you," before it was too late.

Other life events—the birth of a grandchild, the death of a family member, a diagnosis of breast cancer, a financial crisis—can prompt a similar realization that holding on to a hurt is pointless. At times of crisis we see more clearly the miracle of the ordinary. We sense how precious time is and how ridiculous it is to squander time on poisonous thoughts.

Many acts of forgiveness take place when a family member is dying. Death reminds us, more powerfully than anything else, how much family matters. It is wonderful when reconciliation happens before the end—but sad that it so often takes such an event to bring it about. Why post-pone forgiveness until tragedy strikes?

9. *The peace I long for in the world begins with me.* I look at the ongoing conflicts in Africa, Northern Ireland, and the Middle East and long for an end to war, hatred, and killing. Then I see the people in my own family whom I am unwilling to forgive. How can I expect others around the globe to forgive those who torture and kill their families, torch their homes, and force them into refugee camps if I am unwill-ing to deal with my much smaller grievances? In the inter-connected world in which we live, each act of love increases the love in the world, and each act of hate deep-ens hatred globally. The ancient adage that peace begins with me remains fundamentally true.

Forgiving requires generosity and hard work.

Forgiving requires generosity and hard work. It must be anchored in convincing answers to the question, Why forgive? Your own incentives may be among those dis-cussed in this chapter: awareness of God's forgiveness of you or the compelling example of Jesus, recognition of the harm that refusing to forgive inflicts on you and your fam-ily, realization of your love for family members, or con-cern for how your own hardness hinders peace in the wider world. Perhaps you are aware of other promptings not mentioned here. Take time in prayer to find what motivates you, and decide to begin the process of forgive-ness now.

O God,
Your word is life. Help me to forgive.

Opposing forces battle within me, pulling me back and forth as in some game of tug-of-war. I want to forgive. Then suddenly I'm back in the hurt and anger again, and they won't let go.

You are the healer of the human spirit. Guide my steps toward understanding and compassion. Open my eyes to the truth you would have me see. Help me to do what is right.

Thank you for so graciously forgiving me again and again and for the example of your son, Jesus. Let these light my way.

Amen.

Chapter 3

Refusing to Get Even

A certain African tribe captures monkeys by putting food in the bottom of heavy jugs with narrow necks. The monkey smells the food, slips his open hand down the neck of the jug, and closes it around the food. Then he tries to withdraw his hand. He cannot. The hunter easily walks up and captures the monkey—because he won't let go. And so the monkey loses his life.

When we are hurt, we want to settle the score, to return blow for blow. "I really let Paul have it," a woman says. "After what he did to me, it felt so good to tell him what a rotten brother he is." Revenge promises satisfaction and power. Escaping its snare proves difficult. Like the monkey with his hand in the jug, we think that by hanging on we will get what we're after. Letting go doesn't occur to us.

Family revenge takes many forms: withholding information, demanding that family members have nothing to do with the person who hurt us, refusing to attend weddings and graduations, stonewalling attempts to solve a problem. But, whatever its form, revenge fails to deliver on its positive promises. Instead, like heat under boiling oil, it keeps things churning. Family members who pursue revenge become mirror images of what they despise. That is why an ancient Chinese proverb cautions, "The one who pursues revenge should dig two graves."

How do we get beyond this powerful desire to get even? Jesus shows us how. His teaching turns our logic about retaliation upside down. In its place he offers paradox, statements that sound self-contradictory or downright absurd. If you want to hold on to your life, give it away, he says. If someone hits you, turn the other cheek. Instead of trying to even the score with enemies, learn to love them. To finally get free of the resentment that haunts you, forgive the person. Jesus' words about forgiveness sound illogical. Could he be right that his is, in fact, the real way to the happiness and peace we desire?

Even Jesus' first disciples had trouble avoiding the seduction of revenge. When the hour of Jesus' death nears, he is determined to go to Jerusalem. On the way, a village of Samaritans refuses to welcome him.

> When his disciples James and John saw it, they said,
> "Lord, do you want us to command fire to come
> down from heaven and consume them?" (Luke 9:54)

Calling down destruction on enemies has seemed a good solution for centuries. But Jesus rejects this idea. He shows us another way. It involves hard work. His teaching calls for discipline of the instinct to strike back. It puts a restraint on tongue and actions. But it prepares us for the unexpected arrival of grace.

THE ENEMY AS BEARER OF GRACE

In Jesus' time, all it took to conjure up an image of the enemy was to mention a Samaritan. That is why the parable of the Good Samaritan illustrates such a complete reversal of the relationship between Jews and Samaritans. For many years I thought I understood this parable. Among its cast of characters I never saw myself as the priest or Levite, casting furtive glances at the person in the ditch while hurrying to get on with other business. No, I would definitely be the person who stops and binds up the injured person's wounds.

Then I decided to put myself in the predicament of the injured person in the trenches to see how the whole incident appeared from that vantage point. What a shock to look up and see that the person who was about to help me was a Samaritan, someone I considered my worst enemy! "Is anyone else available up there?" I wanted to ask. Or, could it possibly be that this person was to be the conduit of my healing? That was a hard message to swallow. But there was no escaping the paradox of this parable: My enemy may be a source of grace.

A story from the U.S. war in Iraq makes this point powerfully. Members of a Christian Peacemaker Team were making their way from Baghdad to Amman, Jordan. A few hours from the Jordanian border as they traveled at eighty miles an hour to minimize the risk of being bombed, a tire blew on one of their cars. The driver lost control, and the car veered off the road, landing on its side at the bottom of a ten-foot ditch.

My enemy may be a source of grace.

The peacemakers managed to open the doors at the top of the car and eventually got everyone out. But some in their party were badly injured and bleeding. The rest of the convoy had continued on at high speed and were nowhere in sight. Their own car was totaled, and few other vehicles were on the road from Baghdad to Jordan. Just as panic began to set in, an Iraqi civilian stopped to ask if he could help. He packed the injured into his car and drove to Rutba, the closest Iraqi town.

Bombing had destroyed much of Rutba, a town of about twenty thousand people, but the driver took the group to the one medical facility still standing. It was a twenty-by-twenty-foot clinic with four beds. Although three days earlier American and British aircraft had devastated their town, the people warmly welcomed the wounded Americans. An Iraqi doctor who spoke perfect English arrived. He treated one American's gashed head and another's broken bones. The doctor apologized for the clinic's having so few medications and for the fact that bombs had destroyed the ambulance that might have taken the wounded to Jordan.

Two hours later, after everyone had been attended to, the other cars in the peacemakers' convoy arrived to take the injured on to Jordan. Though the Americans tried to pay the clinic and doctor for their care, the Iraqis refused. "We treat everyone in our clinic: Muslim, Christian, Iraqi, or American," the doctor said. "We all are part of the same family, you know."[1]

This incident provides an example of the Gospel parable of the Good Samaritan lived out in the midst of modern war. Most of us will never find ourselves in such extreme circumstances, but stories like this inspire us to move beyond revenge in simple, daily ways. The obstacles on our path to forgiveness seem much less formidable when compared to those faced by the people of Rutba.

To apply this parable to your own family life, consider qualities or actions of relatives that hurt and anger you. See if you can recognize how they might be grace—how a family member who feels like an enemy might become a source of healing. When I try this with my own family, I realize that often the relative who most irritates me throws light on my own blind spots. Does a niece or nephew seem to live too wild a lifestyle? Maybe it is also true that I have pretty rigid rules. Is a sibling shirking family responsibilities? What about my tendency to take over and tell others what to do? Is an in-law too demanding? Perhaps I don't know how to say no. If I can honestly look at my own relational patterns, family pain might lead to growth rather than perpetual bitterness.

SEEKING THE GOOD LIFE INSTEAD OF REVENGE

Baseball provides a lesson in redirecting vengeful feelings. Pitching coaches teach their pitchers that it really does not help to turn around and glare at a fielder who misses a play he or she should have made. Instead, it is much more effective to focus on the positive goal of striking out the next batter. Returning pain for pain does not work, but something else does. Instead of obsessing over a past hurt, we can redirect our energy toward the good things we want.

If we let revenge consume us, we will miss the songs of red-winged blackbirds, the colors of sunsets, and the laughter of friends. An ancient adage maintains that a life well lived is the best revenge. While attempting to strike back at another person proves futile, we have the power to create beauty and happiness for our families and ourselves. We cannot control another person's actions, but we can influence our own. Movement toward goodness balances the scale in a way that revenge never can.

Experiment with this idea for a moment. Notice how tight and constricted you become when you fantasize ways to punish someone who has wronged you. Then redirect your imaginings to gratitude for your blessings. Envision ways to bring about more of what you most value—health, friends, kindness, hope, success, love, community. Observe the peace and expanded energy this exercise brings. When anger toward someone who wronged you makes your sleep fitful and broken, try turning your mind and heart to prayers of gratitude. Begin by giving thanks for each good thing from that day; then move to the larger blessings of your life. When you refuse to pursue revenge and create less vengeful "movies of the mind," you still may experience pain at the injustice of life. Life's unfairness will continue to grate. You will know the price of refraining from retaliation. But you have begun to balance life's harsh realities with its goodness and blessings.

The Hebrew Scriptures contain a story about this seeking of the good life rather than revenge: the account of Joseph and his brothers, found in Genesis 37–50. This tangled tale of family includes crisscrossing love, jealousy, quarrels, anger, plots of revenge, and forgiveness.

Joseph, the favored son of Jacob because he is born in Jacob's old age, makes the mistake of flaunting the long, fancy robe Jacob has made for him. He also tells his brothers about his dreams, visions that show Joseph ruling over them. This infuriates the brothers, who hate him so much they plot to kill him. They manage to ambush Joseph one day when Jacob sends him to visit them at Shechem where they are pasturing the family's flock of sheep. They want to murder him right then, but their brother Judah convinces them to sell Joseph to Midianite slave traders instead, who take him to Egypt. The brothers soak Joseph's robe in goat's blood and take it back to their father as evidence that a wild beast has devoured him.

While in Egypt, Joseph prospers and soon becomes governor of the region. Eventually a severe famine grips the world, and everyone must come to him to buy grain. The famine also strikes hard in his homeland, Canaan. When Joseph's father learns that grain is available in Egypt, he sends ten of his sons there to buy grain. *What*, we wonder, *will Joseph do?* He has good reason to hate his brothers and settle accounts with them now that he has the chance.

At first Joseph feels tempted to pursue revenge. He recognizes his brothers but treats them like strangers, questions them harshly, and puts them in prison for three days. But then something changes in Joseph. Overcome with affection and emotion, he has trouble hiding his weeping. As the story unfolds, he prepares a feast for his brothers and fills their sacks with grain. Finally, he reveals his identity: "I am your brother, Joseph, whom you sold into Egypt. And now do not be distressed, or angry with yourselves, because you sold me here; for God sent me before you to preserve life" (45:4-5).

> *At the heart of forgiveness lies the grace to turn from pursuing revenge.*

Joseph is not perfect. His story contains many sordid aspects. But he endures the cruelty of his brothers and manages to overcome his anger and grief. He withholds vengeance. As in our own stories, his forgiveness happens over time. It is a craft he must learn. His words and actions point to our own path. They suggest ways to embody God's words in the book of Deuteronomy:

I have set before you life and death, blessings and curses. Choose life so that you and your descendants may live. (30:19)

At the heart of forgiveness lies the grace to turn from pursuing revenge, even when revenge so seductively promises justice and happiness. Hate cannot conquer hate; only love can do that. This is the truth that makes us look like fools, all the while leading our families and us into the wisdom of God. We pray to remain open to this divine grace and wisdom.

Dear God,
How patient you are with our failures to love one another, with our desire to seek revenge. Look with compassion on our brokenness. We desperately need your help. Speak your word of light to our darkness and turmoil.

You save us in such mysterious ways. Open us to your redeeming grace. Send your cleansing waters to all those places in us so parched with past pain.

Open our eyes to the wonder of your creation that we may praise your boundless love. Grant us hope in the midst of confusion, and courage to face the truth and follow your call.

Source of endless mercy, refresh our spirits and give us peace.
Amen.

Chapter 4

Dealing with Anger

P at, the older of two sisters, struggled for years to finish her law degree and find a job in a good firm. Her
success pleases her. Though still living at home, she has
carefully managed her money and soon will have her own
apartment. She hopes this makes her mom proud.

The problem, as Pat sees it, is her younger sister.
Carrie never seems to get her act together. She ran with
the wrong crowd in high school and still drinks too much.
Her mom keeps bailing Carrie out, loaning her money
every time she asks.

Take last night, for instance. Carrie had been gone all
weekend, no doubt squandering her paycheck partying

with friends. All day her mom kept peering out the living room window, then running out to the street to see if she could spot Carrie's car at the curve where the road angles toward their house. At midnight, when Carrie finally pulled into the driveway, her mom rushed out to make sure she was OK. Pat watched them embrace, her mom holding Carrie close as Carrie wept and promised not to mess up again.

This made Pat furious. It was so unfair. She never did anything to disappoint her mom, yet she seldom got so much as a word of praise. Meanwhile Carrie, who caused them all endless grief, reaped all the attention. Carrie was clearly her mom's favorite. Pat refused to join in their midnight supper. Instead, she stomped off to her room and slammed the door. Her mom couldn't understand why she wasn't relieved to have Carrie home safe.

This story echoes the New Testament account of the prodigal son (Luke 15:11-32), though I retell it here as the story of a prodigal daughter. In reading this parable we usually focus on the main theme of a wayward child and a forgiving parent. Heard that way, the parable assures us of God's faithful love even when we are at our worst.

But the story has a subplot—a sibling's struggle with resentment at feeling less loved. Hearing the parable, we may identify more with the angry older sibling than with the younger one who is forgiven for squandering the family fortune.

The Bible does not tell us how the parable ends. Does the older child finally join the feast? Experience suggests how hard it is to let go of anger at feeling treated unfairly.

Resentment doesn't simply disappear. We can stomp out of the room, move away, halt all communication, or cut someone out of our lives. But if we do not forgive, the feelings will escalate. Anger, an appropriate immediate response to pain, when unchecked can bind us forever.

Forgiveness frees us from this prison. But it requires solid emotional work. We must process the anger, sadness, and fear arising from a hurt. A first step toward forgiving, and perhaps the hardest one, is recognizing our feelings. The most common, powerful, and complex of these emotions is anger.

> *Anger, an appropriate immediate response to pain, when unchecked can bind us forever.*

LEARNING ABOUT ANGER

Though there are killer strains of it, anger is actually designed to protect us. Anger alerts us to danger. It signals that what we love is threatened—our happiness, the family's survival, justice. It tells us something is wrong in a relationship—for example, that we are receiving abuse and cruelty rather than love and care. Healthy anger provides a helpful response to criticism, rejection, or being ignored. It is, in fact, a gift.

At the physical level, anger is an instinct of self-defense. When we experience or recall a hurt, our body reacts as though it were threatened, going into what is known as a fight-or-flight response. The heart speeds up and blood pressure rises. Muscles tighten and breathing becomes shallow. These and other physiological changes are meant to help us get out of the danger. But they cause endless physical stress if we keep replaying a grievance. Trapped in the anger, we cannot get free enough to make good choices.[1]

Anger, a good and helpful emotion, becomes a problem when we act without taking time to direct its energy well or when we make anger a way of life. We blame our distress on the persons who hurt us and stoke the fires of our resentment toward them. The more we replay the story of how they wronged us, the larger they loom in our imaginations.

> *Anger becomes a problem when we act without taking time to direct its energy well.*

Consider how Kerry's anger toward her niece, Nancy, gradually dominated her life. Nancy's mother, Kerry's favorite sister, had died after a long battle with breast cancer. During her mother's final days, Nancy had refused to let Kerry spend time at her bedside and only called Kerry the morning her sister died. Kerry's rage, fueled by her immense loss, was enormous. She refused to hear Nancy's reasons for what she had done. Instead, she blamed Nancy for all her sorrow and continually rehearsed versions of the events that magnified the wrongness of Nancy's actions. As a result, Nancy loomed ever larger in her life, robbing Kerry of the ability to truly mourn the loss of her sister. Her anger hijacked her, locking her into an endless cycle of blame and pain. How can she get free?

PROCESSING ANGER SAFELY

The time it takes to identify and process feelings depends on the nature and severity of the wound. Some offenses, like abuse or violence, may require years and professional help. Whatever the offense, a fundamental rule for processing anger is this: Do not harm yourself or anyone else. We must learn to manage the physical stimuli that grip us after a hurt. Anger can be as challenging to control as a wild stallion. When wronged, we need to let our emotions subside before acting. This may mean taking a break and removing ourselves physically from the situation. During this time-out, it is important not to replay the offense.

A common tendency is to vent the anger. Venting feels good in the moment. We rage, throw things, scream. Venting takes other forms as well.

> *Contempt:* "That is the lowest thing I've ever seen anyone do."

> *Sarcasm:* "Oh, that's just great. You, who never do a thing around here, are now telling me what to do."

> *Name-calling:* "You are a lazy, worthless liar."

Venting promises to get rid of anger, just as opening a window on a cold day lets heat out. But venting actually keeps the anger coming, generating lots of heat and little light. It escalates the anger at times into violence. Further, initial expressions of anger can be out of proportion or misdirected. When we vent, we become like a wound-up mechanical toy that keeps going until it collapses. The toy has no signal that tells it to stop. It does not know that it is really going nowhere.

If venting doesn't work, what does? Since being strongly angry and fully relaxed at the same time is difficult, deep breathing provides one effective approach to the physical experience of anger. Breathing in and out slowly allows calmer feelings to emerge. A physical outlet also helps: walk, jog, hit tennis balls, use a punching bag, swim, bicycle, draw or paint your anger.

Parents can teach children how to calm down when they are upset. Model this by saying words like these: "I'm feeling very angry right now, so I'm going to take some deep breaths before I do anything else." Show children how to breathe deeply or say calming words to themselves when they are not angry. This will prepare them for when they become upset. We do not have to be perfect at managing our emotions to serve as good examples for children. Even when we fall short of our own standards, we can use that situation to teach. We can apologize, describe our feelings when we vented, and explain how we see the matter now.

Talking about the hurt with one or two supportive persons also works when processing anger. However, help from family and friends can be either productive or nonproductive. Such help functions best when others are honest with us and when we use their help to make changes, not to feed a sense of being right. It is not useful to complain endlessly to family and friends about how poorly we have been treated, to insist that they take our side, and to continue rehearsing the grievance.

Another method of releasing anger is writing a letter that you will not send. Writing reduces the strength of the anger and brings clarity about exactly what happened, what you feel, and why. You write a letter, usually a series of letters, to the family member who has hurt you. In the letter you say all that you want to convey to that person but know that it would be unwise to communicate directly. Here are suggestions for making the process most effective:

1. Place yourself in God's presence as you begin, asking for the healing that you and this person need. Remind yourself that you will not hurt the person or others by writing, since you do not intend to send this letter.

2. Address the person directly by name, just as you would in any letter. You do not need to start with *Dear*, since that word probably does not honestly express your feeling. Pour out all you have to say without editing or censoring yourself. State your message as strongly as you need to.

3. When you feel finished for the time being, delete the letter from your computer or tear it up and dispose of it. Some people burn their letters and mix the ashes with soil in which they plant seeds symbolizing hope for the healing of the relationship.

You may need to write several versions of the letter. Each time begin again; do not revise your previous letter. The process, not the end product, is the point, though you may wind up with a letter you actually want to send. Since this process takes time, you cannot use it for every hurt. But it works well for important matters, including unfinished healing with relatives who have died.

Finally, if your feelings of anger or sadness overwhelm you—if they prevent you from carrying on with normal life, seriously affect your eating and sleeping, or make you feel suicidal—seek help from your doctor or a counselor. You may need medication or psychotherapy to help you deal with your pain. Rage from serious injuries can be too strong to face alone.

TURNING ANGER INTO CREATIVE ACTION

Anger frequently arises when someone fails to meet our need for recognition, acceptance, or belonging. We then have a choice. We can continue trying to get the person to fill those desires, going back repeatedly to remedy the original hurt. Or we can clearly state what we want and find more effective methods of getting it. We can endlessly attempt to right a wrong, or we can let go and direct our energy toward moving on. For example, instead of trying to persuade her grown children to spend more time with her and resenting their many activities, a mother might make new friends herself or pour her energies into causes she cares about.

In this approach to anger, we take responsibility for our lives. Yes, something bad happened to us, but we can still make life-giving choices. In this way forgiveness heals. Too often anger binds us to the offender, turning us into a kite with strings controlled by other hands. When we move forward with God's help, we are no longer held powerless by the wrongdoer.

There is another way to transform anger creatively. When relinquishing resentment seems impossible, we can turn it over to God with short prayers: "Release me from my anger, O God." "Forgive this person, O God; I cannot."

Or we can release anger in a longer meditation. Since the Bible so often uses water as a divine image, I suggest that family members who feel powerless over their rage imagine themselves pouring it into the ocean of God's love, where it can be safely and compassionately absorbed. Passages from the Psalms can accompany this imaging.

> But you do see! Indeed you note trouble and grief,
>   that you may take it into your hands;
> the helpless commit themselves to you. (Psalm 10:14)

> Even though I walk through the darkest valley,
>   I fear no evil;
> for you are with me;
>   your rod and your staff—
>   they comfort me. (Psalm 23:4)

Such prayer reminds us that we need not enter chaos and darkness alone. God is large enough to handle our anger.

SADNESS, FEAR, AND ANGER'S OTHER COMPANIONS

Judith Wallerstein, founder of the Center for Families in Transition, interviewed family members decades after divorce. She found that a third of divorced couples remain intensely angry with their former spouses even ten years later. Caught in the emotional pain of the divorce, they continue to feel humiliation and jealousy over child support battles and new partners. And their children experience the high pitch of their parents' never-dying anger.

Sometimes the problem is the grief beneath the anger.

> *Anger seldom walks alone. It brings other emotional companions like fear and sadness.*

Wallerstein notes that divorce often is precipitated by a serious loss such as the illness of a child, the death of a parent, or the termination of a job. The tragedy splits the family apart. Grief turns to rage as spouses blame each other for failing to understand their pain. Their anger at each other cloaks profound sadness.[2]

Anger seldom walks alone. It brings other emotional companions like fear and sadness. I frequently ask clients, "What would you be feeling if you were not feeling so angry?" Almost always they respond, "Deeply sad." Grief often hurts more than anger. So we cloak it in rage. To be able to forgive we may need to first weep the tears of sorrow. Here the Psalms help once again.

> Turn, O LORD, save my life;
>> deliver me for the sake of your steadfast love. . . .
> I am weary with my moaning;
>> every night I flood my bed with tears;
>> I drench my couch with my weeping.
> My eyes waste away because of grief;
>> they grow weak because of all my foes.
>> (Psalm 6:4, 6-7)

Sometimes clients answer my question about what they would feel if they were not so focused on anger with "very afraid" or "anxious." We reluctantly name these emotions because they seem cowardly and make us vulnerable. Anger defends us against feelings of inadequacy and fear.

Describing exactly what we feel after a hurt is not always easy. Our emotions may be a confusing tangle, changing daily. Listen to some possible layers of emotion and see if a mixture of anger, fear, and sadness names your own condition.

> I can't forgive my uncle for getting drunk at my wedding reception. I had imagined for so long how wonderful my wedding would be, and he ruined it all. Now I'm afraid everyone thinks less of me.

> My mother never took the time to show me she loved me, and now Alzheimer's disease has robbed her of her mind. I'm grieving the mother I never had and now never will. How can I ever forgive her for not showing me love while she still could?

Forgiveness requires us to manage anger, mourn losses, and honestly confront fears. This is not easy. But when we do it in God's presence, grace is there to help us acknowledge and deal with what is going on inside.

WHEN EMOTIONS FLARE UP AGAIN

We intend to forgive for good, but then seeing a certain relative stirs up all the old feelings. Forgiveness may not eliminate our pain once and for all, but these flare-ups usually

become less intense. If emotions resurface, simply acknowledge them and let them go. Recall what the feeling is about
and what you have decided to do with it: "I know I still feel
some hurt about not being invited to my aunt's birthday
party, but I've decided I can accept the fact that I'm not
among her close friends."

Scripture does not suggest that we will never be angry.
Plenty of anger is present in the Bible. Ephesians 4:26 says,
"Be angry but do not sin; do not let the sun go down on
your anger." In other words, learn to identify and process
anger safely. Work with your anger to break it down. Do
not let it harden into hatred and vengeance.

Chapter 5

Who Do I Really Need to Forgive?

We expect the first step in forgiving—recognizing that we are hurt and why—to be fairly straightforward. Someone harmed us, and that is why we are in pain. But human relationships are seldom so simple, especially in the complicated dynamics of family life. We bring complex personal histories to each family encounter. They are woven from past experience, as well as from deeply held convictions about ourselves. That is why we need to ask ourselves, *Who do I really need to forgive?*

FORGIVING OURSELVES

If we take time to sort through the layers of hurt and anger over an incident, we may be surprised to discover that the person we most need to forgive is our self. How can this be? Isn't it clear that the other person is causing our pain? Yes,

We may discover that the person we most need to forgive is our self.

but their actions may be only part of the reason we feel the way we do. For example, a mother resents the fact that her son cannot hold a steady job. But just beneath the surface of her anger lurks the fear that she failed to raise him well. She is embarrassed that her friends know he dropped out of college. At family gatherings she compares herself to the other parents whose children seem so successful. She cannot forgive her son until she can forgive herself for not being the mother she thinks she should be.

Jesus offers us this capacity to forgive ourselves. He sent people away lighter, less burdened by their limitations. After meeting Jesus, they were able to own their sinfulness without denial or harsh judgment. How freeing it was to have at least one person know their faults and still not reject them.

This same grace can reach into our lives when we encounter Jesus in the gospel today. Enter the following passages with openness to that gift.

Become the woman accused of adultery (see John 8:1-11). Your accusers, who want you stoned, shame you. They bring you to Jesus, who is teaching in the Temple. His words to them astonish you: "Let anyone among you who is without sin be the first to throw a stone at her." One by one they slink away, until you stand alone before Jesus. Not a single stone is thrown. Then listen as Jesus speaks his healing words to you: "Has no one condemned you? . . . Neither do I condemn you. Go your way, and from now on do not sin again."

Or imagine you are Zacchaeus, the rich tax collector (see Luke 19:1-10). You are so short that you can't see Jesus because of the crowd, so you climb a sycamore tree to catch a glimpse of him. When Jesus calls you down from the tree and asks to stay at your house, you can hardly believe your ears. You vow to pay back those you have defrauded and give money to the poor. Spend some time experiencing the power of Jesus' forgiveness.

The encounters between Jesus and the woman at the well (John 4:1-42) and the woman who anoints his feet (Luke 7:36-50) likewise illustrate how learning to forgive others is rooted in the grace of being forgiven oneself.

What happens when we learn to accept the unacceptable parts of ourselves? Judgment is no longer our primary attitude toward ourselves and others. More at home with both our good and bad qualities, we can more readily accept that mixture in others. When forgiveness becomes the pattern for relating to ourselves, we can more easily extend forgiveness to others. As in learning to skate or bicycle, we soon repeat the movements of forgiveness as though they were the most natural way to move about in the world.

Sometimes the very act of forgiving another opens the way to self-forgiveness. Like a set of Russian nesting dolls where each reveals yet another doll inside, each act of forgiveness releases another. A man describing this experience says that until he forgave his mother, self-forgiveness was never an issue for him. He did not think he had done anything wrong; he blamed everything on her. Forgiving his mother allowed him to be honest about himself.

> I saw that, yeah, I was involved with drugs, I was mean to her, I was cruel. . . . So that brought me to feeling . . . remorseful for what happened and my involvement in it.[1]

We commonly tend to consider ourselves innocent and others wrong. As the Gospel says, we fix our attention on the splinter in another's eye, while we completely ignore the long piece of lumber in our own (Matt. 7:1-5). Like a robin guarding her nest or a mother bear watching for any danger to her cubs, our first reactions are defensive. We blame, then try to fix, the other person. In fact, the person who forgives is the first one changed by the act of forgiveness.

LETTING OURSELVES BE LOVED

Many situations of forgiveness call for mutual repentance and release. Both parties have said and done things they regret. But asking for forgiveness implies guilt. It means acknowledging that one is wrong. Feelings of unworthiness or self-hatred get in the way of this admission. When my husband and I try to find our way through a painful incident, I know it would help if I could fully admit my failures instead of skirting the issue. But I have trouble getting those words of ownership out there, naming my part in the hurt and misunderstanding. Doing so threatens my sense of being a good person. The more I believe that I am lovable, the more I can accept responsibility for my role in the misunderstanding.

The way we respond to interpersonal wounding often depends on how we feel about ourselves. Compared to the rest of the family, we may judge ourselves as not very beautiful, clever, talented, or intelligent. Somehow we fail to measure up. A friend sums this up in talking about her relationship with her sister: "When I'm feeling bad about myself, I'm angry with her. When I'm feeling good about myself, I can afford to forgive her." If we feel unloved and unlovable, we may see hurt where none is intended.

Forgiveness is easier if we have learned to open ourselves to God's love. When you ponder whether to forgive others, take a moment to imagine God's loving you just as you are, with all your goodness and all your limitations. Breathe in that love, allowing it to reach all the dark places inside you. Feel it wash over you like a cleansing rain. Then listen to biblical reminders of God's love like these from the prophets.

> Can a woman forget her nursing child,
>   or show no compassion for the
>   child of her womb?
> Even these may forget,
>   yet I will not forget you. (Isaiah 49:15)

Yet it was I who taught Ephraim to walk,
   I took them up in my arms;
   but they did not know that I healed them.
I led them with cords of human kindness,
   with bands of love.
I was to them like those who lift infants
   to their cheeks.
   I bent down to them and fed them.

                              (Hosea 11:3-4)

Loving-kindness is the practice of sending blessings to various beings, beginning with ourselves.

In the immediate emotional heat of a hurt, praying these passages may not be possible, but as feelings calm down, reading such selections from scripture can help us act from a place grounded in self-love.

If children are to learn forgiveness, above all they need love—the kind of love that fosters a positive self-concept, a sense of worth, and inner strength. We first experience God's love and forgiveness through the love of our parents. When children develop their talents and gifts and receive praise and appreciation, they learn they have value as persons. This knowledge prepares them to see the needs and worth of others. When they feel good about themselves, they can more easily treat others with kindness.

Christianity and many other religious traditions stress the link between love of self and love of others. The first time I read the Buddhist prayer for loving-kindness, I was struck by the fact that it begins with *me*, not with the one I consider my enemy.

Loving-kindness is the practice of sending blessings to various beings in the universe, beginning with ourselves. Wishing another person well starts with wishing oneself well. The practice usually opens with an expression of forgiveness like the following.

> I ask forgiveness of all beings whom I have hurt or harmed in any way. I freely forgive all beings who have hurt or harmed me in any way. I freely forgive myself.

You can then speak any blessings you choose. Usually four or five is considered a helpful number. Repeat these blessings again and again.

> May I be safe from inner and outer danger.
> May I be happy and peaceful in mind.
> May I be strong and healthy in body.
> May I tend my life with happy ease.[2]

After praying these blessings for yourself, you can direct them to other family members, substituting *you* or the person's name for *I*. For example, the first blessing becomes, "May you be safe from inner and outer danger." To make this practice feel more genuine, put the blessings in your own words: "May my sister, who irritates me, get relief from her fear and worries." "May my granddaughter, who uses drugs, accept help and stay out of worse trouble."

When praying for others, it helps to begin with persons we feel closest to and gradually work our way to the more difficult relationships. Praying for others does not necessarily erase anger and resentment, but it does make hanging onto hatred impossible. Further, the grace of such prayer takes us wherever we need to go next in our relationships with them.

TRIGGERING OLD PAIN

Pondering who we really need to forgive leads not only to the nooks and crannies of the self but to past events that cast a shadow over the present. Thumbing through old family photos summons up memories of special times: summer vacations and family reunions, weddings and birthdays, proud parents and siblings mugging for the camera. So many snapshots of ties of the heart.

But not all family memories are happy. Many are painful and sad. We carry traces of events we barely remember or desperately want to forget: the death of a loved one, chronic illness, miscarriages, suicides, neglect, abuse, loud arguments, alcohol-driven scenes, ridicule, deceit. Long after we leave home, these events remain a part of us.

We sometimes wonder why such a small thing—a relative's passing remark, facial expression, or attempt at humor—triggers so much rage or sadness in us. When feelings related to a present hurt seem out of proportion to what roused them, it is likely we are borrowing energy from old family wounds. Like an oil spill that coats shorelines and birds, past pain seeps into the currents and eddies of our present life.

Take Wendy. She grew up in a home where her parents constantly compared her large frame with her sister's petite body. Wendy later marries and joins a family where all the women are health enthusiasts. When they get together for summer vacations, Wendy bristles at any mention of weight and size, seeing it as a reflection on her. She cannot forgive the insensitivity of her husband's family, she says, and refuses to attend any more of these gatherings. She is sure her in-laws are indirectly making fun of her with all their talk about exercise and weight-loss programs.

Are Wendy's in-laws really the problem? Whom does she actually need to forgive? If Wendy can name how these family gatherings tap into her own past pain, she may come to like this new family she has joined. Or she may stay locked in former resentments. One way for her to get free of them is to acknowledge her anger about being compared with her sister. Wendy suffers from a twenty-year-old wound. She needs help to heal these memories.

Or consider a child who cares for a chronically ill parent, then turns into an overly responsible adult. A perfectionist and people-pleaser, she carries many burdens and resents the lack of appreciation she receives from other family members.

When we find ourselves easily hurt or resentful, it helps to ask, *What does this situation remind me of?* In our attempts to forgive, we often uncover not just a single incident but a series of hurts. When we try to forgive one person, we realize there are others we also need to forgive. Taking time to sort through our emotions clarifies the sources of our pain and guides us more surely toward the action we need to take.

Chapter 6

Changing Habits of the Heart

Cardiologists tell us that when the physical heart hardens, it becomes inflexible and loses its ability to move life-giving blood. It can no longer send nurturing elements to other parts of the body. Increasing disability and disease gradually take their toll on the entire body.

Something similar happens to a family's spiritual health when members refuse to forgive. Closed hearts cannot receive or give sustenance.

Check out your own heart. Does it contain messages like the following, engraved in stone?

I will never speak to him again.

If you do that, don't ever plan on coming home.

She will never change, so I will have nothing to do with her.

Heart hardening occurs when people repeat statements that lock them into one position. You couldn't pry open such hearts with a crowbar. Nothing new can find its way in.

But there is hope for healing. God has promised to break open our hearts. New insights from within and from without enable us to understand our wounding and to break free of its grip. In the power of the Spirit, we form new habits of the heart.

> I will give them one heart, and put a new spirit within them; I will remove the heart of stone from their flesh and give them a heart of flesh. (Ezekiel 11:19)

The challenge is to remain receptive to the Spirit's redeeming action. Here are two ways to do that.

Stop Going Over the Hurt

The initial response to a hurt is spontaneous. After that, we play a part in keeping our feelings stirred up. We turn over in our minds each detail of the injury, adding inflammatory interpretations for good measure. We blame the other person for what we are experiencing and minimize any fault of our own. The urge to nurse and magnify a wound is as strong as a craving for chocolate.

My sister never thinks of anyone but herself, and this latest move of hers just proves it.

There my mother goes again, sticking her nose into my business. Just like that time three years ago when I wanted to buy a new house. She has to control everything.

We all talk to ourselves throughout the day, and these inner dialogues wrap our hearts more and more tightly around a hurt. They also magnify and distort the hurt, enlarging an incident by drawing to it all previous slights, like a magnet picking up every bit of metal in the vicinity. This makes it increasingly hard to forgive offending persons, since we build such a convincing case that no reasonable jury could find them anything but guilty as charged.

Forgiveness starts with refusing to rehearse the hurt continually.

Forgiveness starts with refusing to rehearse the hurt continually. An ancient Zen tale illustrates this truth. Two Buddhist monks on their way to a monastery reach a river. On the bank sits a beautiful woman, unable to cross because the water is too high. So one of the monks lifts her onto his back and carries her across.

As the monks continue on their journey, one of them berates the other for his action. He speaks at length about how his companion shouldn't have carried the woman across the river. What would people say? Had he forgotten the Holy Rule about never touching a woman? After listening for some time to the never-ending reproaches, the first monk says: "Brother, I dropped that woman at the river. Are you still carrying her?"[1]

One way to stop rehashing an offense is to substitute prayer for negative thoughts. Such prayer embodies ancient Christian wisdom about how our inner world gets distorted and about how to straighten it out. We find these brief prayers in many places: favorite hymns, biblical passages, treasured sayings, or names for God. They can be very simple: "God, help me." "God, fill me with your love." "Spirit of Jesus, free me."

If no prayers of your own occur to you, try breathing in and out as you speak these phrases from the Psalms:

> Have mercy on me, O God,
>   according to your steadfast love. (51:1)

> God is our refuge and strength,
>   a very present help in trouble. (46:1)

> Create in me a clean heart, O God,
>   and put a new and right spirit within me.
>   (51:10)

Prayers like these turn our attention away from the hurt and the offending family member. They bring about inner stillness, replacing negative thinking with hopeful words of faith. They draw us toward God's perspective and remind us that we need God's help to stop clinging to injuries.

Praying for family members on a regular basis also fosters a spirit of forgiveness we can draw on in tough times. Here is one way to do that: Gather some individual or group pictures of your family. Ask other family members, including children, to join you if you like. Light a candle and lay out the photographs. You might even want to pray with a photo album. Recall that you are in the presence of the God who made each of us with love and embraces us with compassion. Slowly focus on each person in the pictures, trying to regard each one with the divine Creator's appreciation for that individual's struggles, gifts, and contributions to the family. Close with a favorite prayer or hymn.

Praying for family members fosters a spirit of forgiveness.

Put Yourself in the Other Person's Shoes

Walking a mile in another person's moccasins isn't easy in the first heat of emotion. However, as time goes by, it becomes possible to see an experience from the standpoint of the family member we are trying to forgive. We may then realize that the person did the best he or she could under the particular circumstances. For example, adult children often decide to forgive their parents after trying to rear their own children. They see that they too fail in spite of their best efforts; they hurt their children no matter how hard they try not to. Their love is imperfect, just like that of their parents. Jesus' words from the Sermon on the Mount challenge anew: "Do not judge, so that you may not be judged" (Matt. 7:1).

All human interacting is ambiguous. We can't always know what another person thinks, feels, or intends. In fact, not even those closest to us fully grasp how life appears from our perspective. As a result, our understanding of a situation may or may not be accurate, and we may take offense when no wrong was intended. Breakthroughs sometimes occur when we can accept the offender as having his or her own inadequacies and unhealed hurts. This realization leads to compassion for the person and insight into ourselves.

Family interactions resemble a visual perception puzzle: if you look at it one way, you see a vase; if you look at it another way, you see two faces. Whichever pattern you see, it is almost impossible, at first glance, to see the other. During years of counseling I have been struck by how completely different two people's accounts of the same situation can be. It may therefore help to ask ourselves: *From all I know about this person, how might he or she see the same incident? What history do I know, or could I learn, that might help me better understand this person?*

> *Breakthroughs sometimes occur when we can accept the offender as having his or her own inadequacies and unhealed hurts.*

Try placing yourself in God's presence and imagine a conversation between yourself and the other person. Go back and forth several times between your accusations and the person's defense, and see if your feelings change as you imagine what the other person might say. Although this is a tough assignment, even attempting it reveals cracks in our conviction that we are entirely innocent while our offender is totally to blame.

We can help children develop the ability to empathize by teaching them to notice the feelings of others. For example, when a child plays with other children, we might ask questions like these: "Look at Sally's face; she's crying. A wave came in and washed part of her sand castle away. How do you think she feels? Do you think you could do something to help her?" Such empathy training begins to instill sensitivity to the feelings of others, an essential component of forgiving.

In *My First White Friend: Confessions on Race, Love, and Forgiveness*, Patricia Raybon releases some of her anger toward her father when she learns more about his own childhood. Her father, she says, was a good man, a steady provider and moral presence who taught her the scriptures, the Apostles' Creed, and his own creed. He paid for orthodontia, college tuitions, summer vacations, and countless other blessings. He also taught his daughters how to survive in America, telling them they needed to be better than white people so that white people couldn't find anything wrong with them, hard as they might try.

Raybon worked mightily to please her father, but she resented his critical eye that so often saw the need for still more improvements. She wanted to be enough for him, to be loved just for who she was. Although her father showed his love for her by all he did for the family, he never could say, "I love you." She heard what he did say to her as evidence that she was flawed, never quite good enough.

Raybon's healing came when she realized that this was exactly how her father was raised. She finally understood that he was trying to toughen her and get her ready for the harsh white spotlight. He believed white people would never find her fully acceptable, so he pushed her to perfection. That was how far he had been pushed. Raybon's efforts to understand her father's pain and fears read like a long reflection on Jesus' words as he was dying on the cross: "Father, forgive them; for they do not know what they are doing" (Luke 23:34).[2]

The insights Raybon reached are the goal of a form of family therapy called *family of origin work*. In this kind of therapy, a family comes together to learn more about the situation in which past pain occurred. Often it involves an adult child meeting with his or her parents. When parents get the opportunity to tell their own story—for example, how they were dealing with alcoholism, job loss, or mental illness during a period when the child felt neglected— the sharing often changes the adult child's understanding of past experience. It does not take away responsibility for the wrong; a parent could have acted otherwise. Nor does it deny the damage that resulted. It does help the child understand that the parent is not simply a wrongdoer but a complex person trying to cope with challenging situations. After hearing the parents' stories, the adult child has a more complete picture of them.

Terry Hargrave, a psychologist who works with families and writes about family forgiveness, tells how he did his own family of origin work around the abuse he experienced as a child. When he finally summoned the courage to talk with his mother, he learned that similar abuse went back generations in her own family. She told him about her own mother and her mother's mother and their inability to give care and nurture: "I just never realized how important it was to hold and love children. I didn't know you were supposed to rock and cuddle babies. It simply did not occur to me that security given by touch was important." Hargrave began to see his parents with new eyes. Compared to what they had experienced, they were in fact good parents. The more he understood about their circumstances while growing up, the more his trust grew.[3]

Changing hearts of stone may seem impossible at first. But here the oyster can serve as a parable for us. The oyster holds a grain inside itself, which is irritating. Over time it bathes itself continually with secretions. Gradually these baths result in a magnificent pearl. In the same way, the two practices we have discussed—substituting prayer for the rehashing of grievances and attempting to see offenders in their own context—slowly create in us a new heart.

My God,
Life's hurts have shut down my heart, binding it with invisible threads of misunderstanding and resentment. They stifle my joy, limit my freedom, and curtail my gratitude.

Yet I know that you want to release me the way your son, Jesus, freed Lazarus from the tomb. Unbind my heart and restore me to my friends and family. Open my eyes to the wonders of your creation, and fill me again with joy and gladness.

You are my rock and my salvation. I count on your steadfast love.

Amen.

Chapter 7

It Often Happens by Inches

S ome years ago I heard a story about how small actions
can bring about large changes. I return to it often for
inspiration when I work with families struggling to forgive
and reconcile. As the tale opens, two birds, a dove and a
coal-mouse, perch on the slim branch of a tree one winter's day. They begin to speak.

> "Tell me the weight of a snowflake," a coal-mouse
> asked a wild dove.
> "Nothing more than nothing," was the answer.

"In that case, I must tell you a marvelous story," the coal-mouse said.

"I sat on the branch of a fir, close to its trunk, when it began to snow—not heavily, not in a raging blizzard—no, just like in a dream, without a wound and without any violence. Since I did not have anything better to do, I counted the snowflakes settling on the twigs and needles of my branch. Their number was exactly 3,741,952. When the 3,741,953rd dropped onto the branch, nothing more than nothing, as you say—the branch broke off."

Having said that, the coal-mouse flew away.

The dove, since Noah's time an authority on the matter, thought about the story for awhile and finally said to herself, "Perhaps there is only one person's voice lacking for peace to come to the world."[1]

The same is true of peace in families. Perhaps all that is missing is one word or action. Simple gestures accumulate like snowflakes, each adding its weight to the healing process. Tentative and partial at first, peace gradually grows stronger.

We may think that forgiveness must be 100 percent to make a difference, like an A+ on a perfect paper. In that case, we reason, it is useless to try. There is no way we can reach that goal. But, in fact, moving toward 50 percent or even 10 percent counts. There are degrees of forgiveness. The key is to start somewhere and to keep trying.

There are degrees of forgiveness. The key is to start somewhere and to keep trying.

Decide not only what you can't do but what you can do. Here are some small steps to consider.

ENTERTAIN THE POSSIBILITY

> "Forgive him? You've got to be kidding! I couldn't possibly do that."

> "Not her! Never. She's got to realize what she did to me."

I hear responses like these when I suggest that forgiveness might provide a way out of personal and family misery. I hesitate at times even to introduce the word. However, forgiveness, always a fundamental Christian ideal, is coming into its own in the field of counseling. Even therapists who dismissed it in the past recognize forgiveness as not only a religious goal but also a powerful path to physical and emotional well-being.

When we experience especially painful wounds, it may be a while before we can bear to hear the word *forgiveness*, but the time comes when we are ready. Speaking of cruel treatment from a relative, a woman says: "I'm not in any hurry to forgive. I have no agenda in that regard. But I do notice a softening of my anger. Something is forgiven inside me. It's more of a grace than something I will to happen. I'm not directing my energy toward him so much anymore."

While it is not our place to tell others they must forgive, we ourselves can entertain the possibility at any moment and see where it takes us. The first step may be the realization that we are now strong enough that the person cannot hurt us anymore. Or we may start to feel some small amount of empathy. We can build on these small beginnings.

GIVE FAMILY MEMBERS CREDIT FOR TRYING

We owe it to others to allow them a fresh start. People can and do change. A daughter remembers her father's relentless criticism as she grew; now she sees him softening as he ages. "He is trying really hard. He's less competitive and angry. What I appreciate is that he keeps coming back to the table to talk again." Or a mother says of her daughter: "I can't quite trust that she has changed. But I keep telling myself, 'She's trying. Just meet her there.'"

People deserve credit for their past deeds as well. Recall something good about the relationship; acknowledge one positive quality in the person. Perhaps the in-law who hurt you was there for you when you needed help after surgery. When relatives recognize one another's efforts, goodwill gradually builds.

PRAY FOR FAMILY MEMBERS IN CONFLICT

We don't always think of praying for family members locked in a dispute. When we hear that a brother is divorcing or two sisters aren't speaking, we may get caught up in taking sides. Instead we can lift them up to God, sending each one love and strength in the Spirit. Such prayers might go something like this:

May the wisdom of the Spirit be with each of you.

May your hearts be open to the grace of healing.

O God, our refuge, protect and guide them.

God of love, show them the way to love.

Prayer addresses the helplessness we feel when our family seems to be unraveling. Each time we hear more of the pain and impasse, we can take the matter to prayer once again.

TAKE ADVANTAGE OF OPPORTUNITIES THAT ARISE

"Sometimes something good comes from something bad," a grandmother tells me. When illness or misfortune strikes, a family has a chance to be there for a member who may believe that no one cares. New situations are also possible when a family member gets treatment for diseases like depression and alcoholism. A man comments that his brother is so much easier to relate to now that he is on medication for chronic depression: "He was hypersensitive and held grudges we didn't even know about. He was always angry, and now he's not angry anymore." When individual members choose health, a family can find it as well.

Several years ago I worked with a woman who came to our nursing center convinced that she was completely alone in the world and would die that way. However, when I told several nieces and nephews of her predicament, they came through for her. In the months before her death, they visited regularly. They were at her bedside around the clock in her final days.

These nieces and nephews had matured over the years, and they no longer took for granted the interest their aunt had taken in them and the money she had spent on their educations. She, in turn, was able to let go of her resentment over being neglected. Her forgiveness allowed her to die in peace and brought healing to several generations of her family.

Restoration of a relationship is sometimes much more partial than this. In his memoir, *An American Requiem: God, My Father, and the War That Came Between Us,* James Carroll movingly describes such an experience. His father was an air force lieutenant general. James became a priest, his father's pride and joy. Then he protested the Vietnam War. His and his father's strong opposing stances on the war tore apart their family. Years later his father was diagnosed with Alzheimer's disease. At the end, James sat with him for hours, the tension between them now gone, the bad feelings a part of the past. Though his father no longer recognized him, James shaved and bathed him, told him stories, and talked about a novel he was writing. His father listened without being offended. James concludes, "It was the next best thing to being reconciled."[2]

LOWER YOUR EXPECTATIONS OF OTHERS

Family members hold one another to high standards of behavior. Lowering these expectations leaves room for forgiveness. What does our accumulated wisdom tell us about family life? Family will not meet all our needs, even some important ones. Family members will make mistakes and sin. Not all family members will like one another or be best friends. Conflict is a normal part of relationships. Every family experiences crisis from time to time.

Most families include the chronic complainers, the relentlessly critical, the boring, the demanding, and the self-absorbed. There are those who cannot listen and those who are too quiet to suit us. We likely fall into several of these categories ourselves. Accepting this fact can relieve much stress and disappointment.

High expectations are the seedbed of harsh judgment. We cannot forgive those who fail to measure up. It helps to turn expectations into preferences, hopes, wishes, or desires: "I would prefer that you be more positive." "I would like it better if you got here on time." "I hope you will get a job soon."

If we can let go, we can enjoy family more. Wisdom entails knowing how to adjust to certain realities that will not change. Wisdom is also knowing what to overlook.

CONTINUE SENDING CARDS, CALLS, AND E-MAILS

A frozen relationship seldom thaws all at once. More often it is a slow melt. For example, a woman sends her sister-in-law an invitation to her daughter's baptism, even though the rest of the family usually excludes her from family events. A daughter announces a small breakthrough in relating to her mother: "I'm so proud of myself. I called my mother last Sunday. I'd been secretly planning to do it for some time, but I didn't tell anyone. I didn't want to feel like I *had* to do it." She goes on to say that she called when she knew her mom would have company arriving shortly; she did not want it to be a long call that would get them both into old patterns. She had managed to reconnect with her mother, but she had set a boundary. She feels pleased with her progress.

When we send news or photos, call, or write, we convey the message that we want a connection with this person. We keep the door open.

PRACTICE THE ART OF LISTENING

Hurts leave us eager to make our own points. Feeling heard and understood, however, generally leads to reconciliation. Listening is an act of caring, and we can offer it to others even when we do not feel any love for them. A daughter, on returning from a visit with her father, said: "It went better this time. I realized that in the past I was too busy judging to be able to really hear him." Even persons we dislike can be the object of this kind of respect, the same respect we hope to receive from them.

> *We can listen to others even when we do not feel any love for them.*

These small moments make peace possible in families. It would be wonderful if forgiveness and reconciliation occurred instantaneously and lasted forever. The time and effort they take discourage us. But throughout the Gospels small things matter; they become the seeds of larger moments of grace.

> With what can we compare the kingdom of God, or what parable will we use for it? It is like a mustard seed, which, when sown upon the ground, is the smallest of all the seeds on earth; yet when it is sown it grows up and becomes the greatest of all shrubs, and puts forth large branches, so that the birds of the air can make nests in its shade. (Mark 4:30-32)

The Gospel reassures us that our efforts, though seemingly insignificant, open us to the movement of the Spirit. The important thing is to begin, trusting the rest to God's promise of transformation.

Short biblical passages can help sow the seeds of forgiveness in family life. Try using some of the following verses at family meals or as morning or evening prayers. Different family members might take turns reading them or select others they would like included.

Do not fear, for I have redeemed you;
  I have called you by name, you are mine. (Isaiah 43:1)

Lord, you have been our dwelling place in all generations.
Before the mountains were brought forth,
  or ever you had formed the earth and the world,
  from everlasting to everlasting you are God.
                    (Psalm 90:1-2)

It was you who formed my inward parts;
  you knit me together in my mother's womb.

I praise you, for I am fearfully and wonderfully made.
  Wonderful are your works; that I know very well.
                                        (Psalm 139:13-14)

On the day I called, you answered me,
  you increased my strength of soul. (Psalm 138:3)

Chapter 8

Reconciliation

I t happened more than twenty years ago, but the memory remains vivid. I was working in a large nursing center. One of our residents, near death from a neurological disease, told me that she wanted to say good-bye to her sister. Would I help her? They had not spoken for twenty-two years. She no longer recalled what their final quarrel had been about.

I managed to locate her sister, who had incurable colon cancer, in another care facility nearby. I set about trying to arrange a visit. Despite all obstacles, the day finally came when the sister arrived at our center. I wheeled her up to my patient's room. One final challenge was maneuvering their wheelchairs so that the sisters could be close to each other. Then I stepped out into the hallway and left them alone.

As I waited, I imagined them talking about the reasons for their estrangement and telling each other how sorry they were. When I glanced into the room after a few moments, I saw that I was wrong. The two sisters were simply leaning forward in their wheelchairs, holding each other and weeping.

Not all reconciliation among family members takes this long or occurs in such a powerful way. But it always carries the same healing. Some missing part of us slips back into place. A feeling of harmony and unity is restored. Although we can forgive without getting back together with a person—and sometimes this is necessary—restored relationships are what we most desire. We are not isolated individuals, with relationships added on as an afterthought. No, our relationships make us who we are.

Geographical distance makes it easier for families today to go on with their lives without mending fences. But the loss of ongoing family relationships hurts, and it puts each succeeding generation at risk. Living without the enduring emotional connections that family provides and that we hunger for exacts a high price.

While forgiveness is a matter of letting go and can be done alone, getting back together again takes two. Both persons must be ready to acknowledge what happened, experience the pain of the rupture, and want to recon-nect. When each keeps an open heart, watches for signs of trust, and takes small steps toward the other, reconciliation becomes possible. The following questions commonly arise in the process.

Where do I begin? What can we learn from families who reconcile? They find creative ways to break out of an impasse. Here are examples of some initial steps.

- A man knows he will meet his former wife at a class reunion. Ten years have passed since their divorce. In his heart he has determined that he needs to say something to her, but he does not know what it will be. When he meets her at the opening banquet, he simply wishes her well and apologizes for the pain he caused. She weeps.

- A daughter who wants to stay connected to her alcoholic parents still calls them but not in the evening when they most likely have been drinking. This spares her the ugly conversations that used to take place at that time.

- A brother who has been estranged from his family for years because he does not feel he can hold his own in their large gatherings starts with a breakfast invitation to the sister he feels most comfortable contacting.

- A woman realizes that relatives who hurt her will attend a family funeral. She must decide how she will act when she sees them. There are, she decides, parts of the relationships that are OK, and she will go with those parts. That means limiting how much of herself she can trust to share with them, but it enables her to be cordial and welcoming on a more basic level.

These confidence-building efforts can restore trust. We often dread seeing someone who has hurt us. Initial steps by family members show that there are different diving boards for taking the leap into the icy waters of a strained relationship. The initial move might be simply getting together for a baseball game, a play, or some other public activity where we spend time together with a focus other than our relationship. We can overlook a behavior we dislike or refrain from saying hurtful words.

Family gatherings provide a natural occasion for reaching out. We may acknowledge our dislike of a family member we have forgiven but relate to that person nonetheless. That realization, in turn, often brings out the best in the other person, increasing his or her attractiveness. It also recognizes a truth about relationships: every person in our lives has both pleasing and irritating traits.

Should I wait for an apology? A sincere apology works wonders in the reconciliation process. It indicates recognition that a person has wronged us. Our anger lessens; defensiveness recedes; goodwill begins to breathe again.

Sometimes an apology comes in a form other than words. A sister bakes cookies and brings them by our house. A husband mows the lawn and takes out the garbage. These legitimate ways of saying, "I'm sorry" may be the only kind of apology some people can manage. At times no apology occurs, but somehow it becomes clear that we can trust the other person once again. We need not wait for the actual words "I'm sorry."

On the matter of apologies we need to remember that many hurts are mutually inflicted. Each person has done something wrong and suffered a hurt; feelings are therefore mixed. If a husband has an affair, he hurts his wife. But she may also have done hurtful things to him, such as turning the children against him. Both need to acknowledge their actions and receive forgiveness. Even when one offense is more serious than another, a situation frequently calls for mutual apologies and forgiveness.

A more daily example of this occurs in heated arguments where both parties lash out with hurtful words. When each shares some guilt, a sincere apology helps. My husband, Tom, is especially good at this. Even when he is not as much to blame as I am, he finds a way to say he is sorry for what he did and wants us to get past it. When we lead marriage enrichment events for couples, we include a simple ritual of forgiveness for the couple to do. Each says in turn, "I have hurt you by _____, and I am sorry." The other replies, "I forgive you as God has forgiven us both." This exercise puts reconciliation in the context of faith.

Do we need to talk about what happened and get the facts straight? When people attempt to reconcile, their conversation can sound like trying to balance a checkbook down to the last penny. Every human interaction is complex and remembered differently. Listening to how each party views the misunderstanding may be important, but trying to determine exactly what happened and who was right and who was wrong often just heats up the old argument again. Is revisiting all this really that crucial?

I used to think that talking things through was necessary to restoring a relationship, and it can be. But another strategy that may work is to let time do its healing and put the breach behind you. For serious issues that need to be addressed and dealt with, a mediator or counselor can help prevent further hurt or a blowup. Sometimes family members can serve as mediators. The difference between mediating and meddling is not always clear, but there is one. Mediators try not to take sides. They attempt to bring the parties together, to facilitate communication, and to keep emotions from getting out of hand.

Prayer serves as vital preparation for these discussions, whatever the setting. This prayer may be used before tough conversations:

> O God, I come to you today because I'm anxious as I get ready for this conversation. I know I have to go through with it, though everything in me wants to avoid it.
>
> I don't really know what to say, and I'm afraid I'll make things worse, lose my temper, or not be able to get my ideas across. But most of all, I'm fearful that I'll hear bad things about myself and the things I've done.
>
> It seems easier just to let the misunderstanding and distance continue. But I know that is not what you ask of me. Send your Spirit to give me courage. Help me find the right words. Give me the grace to listen, learn, and let go.
>
> Teach me to approach this exchange with an open and compassionate heart like that of your son, Jesus. Help me bear pain and disappointment as he did. Be with me. I trust in your wisdom and love.

What if the other person isn't willing to work on the relationship? Full reconciliation requires two people, each of

whom is doing his or her own healing work. We can forgive someone even if he or she remains closed, but we cannot reconcile with that person. Suppose a daughter wants
to heal the breach with her mother, who refused to come
to her wedding. Though raised in a strict Jewish household,
the daughter married a man with no religious faith. As
time passes the daughter works hard to understand her
mother's behavior. She is ready to let go of her pain and
wants to be part of her family again. But her mother has
not done any such forgiving. She still thinks her daughter
was wrong and should have lis-
tened to her advice about whom to
marry. "She married him just to
spite me," the mother keeps telling
herself. Nothing new can happen
between the two until the mother
addresses her own issues and
becomes willing to let go of her
hurt and anger.

> *Full
> reconciliation
> requires two
> people, each of
> whom is doing
> his or her own
> healing work.*

Ending a rift calls for both real-
ism and perseverance. Continue to
send cards and e-mails, or make
occasional phone calls. This action
indicates that you are not hanging on to the hurt and are
open to relating when the other person is ready. Once when
a relative and I were not on good terms, I sent her a birthday card every year. It was my way of saying that I hoped
we could eventually fix what was wrong with our relationship and that I still valued her as a family member. People
change. What is impossible now may well be possible later.

Will we just go back to the same old patterns? We don't have to. That's not what Jesus had in mind when he talked about reconciliation. Reconciliation offers a fresh beginning. Trust must be restored, and this usually occurs in small increments. It helps to look at what patterns we set and find ways to avoid the same old traps. For example, if a nephew borrows cash with no intention of paying it back, he likely will do it again. Disagreements involving money are common triggers for ongoing hostility. Adding the creditor-debtor arrangement to a family connection strains the relationship. First see how you might need to adjust your own behavior. This could mean turning down requests for money, making the money a gift, or drawing up a binding legal document with clear terms.

Old patterns are hard to break, but grace works in the darkness of relational pain. Miracles happen. Consider Marie. She saw her marriage end in a huge fight on Christmas Eve. Her husband, Joe, had once again become drunk and said ugly things. In the heat of anger and alcohol, Joe was his worst self. But losing his marriage shocked him into awareness of what he had become. He entered addiction treatment, did follow-up counseling, and developed spiritual and emotional supports. Over the years he began to face up to the pain he had caused his ex-wife and children. Not only did he ask their forgiveness, but he learned to manage his anger and respond differently to stressful events. Marie and Joe eventually became good friends again, though they never remarried. The whole family felt healing from this reconciliation. Joe was able to give his grandchildren the nurture he never could show his own children.

What if the person repeats the offense? Don't be too surprised. In hurts stemming from the ordinary give-and-take of family life, you probably will have to forgive relatives again and again. The Gospel estimates the number to be seventy-seven times, or always (Matt. 18:21-22). But some repeated injuries are more serious. In these cases reconciliation may not be possible unless the offender makes changes. As we will discuss in the next chapter, you may need to remove yourself from the abusive or dangerous behavior. Sometimes trust is not warranted.

> *Old patterns are hard to break, but grace works in the darkness of relational pain. Miracles happen.*

When restoring family relationships seems impossible no matter what we do, God's Word offers hope beyond our limited efforts, the promise of a future redemption. To reconcile in the biblical sense involves binding up again all that is broken in this world through sin. Reconciliation promises to restore all fractured relationships between human beings, between humans and nature, and between humans and God. Many biblical images convey this hope: The peace of Eden will be restored. There will be a large and joyful banquet. God will wipe away every tear and put an end to weeping and sorrow. On this vast sea of God's love, our family and its story floats.

> They will not hurt or destroy
> on all my holy mountain;

for the earth will be full of the knowledge
    of the LORD
as the waters cover the sea. (Isaiah 11:9)

Family pain and joy are held in a love larger than we can envision. In the lifelong work of healing family brokenness, we glimpse in hope this future possibility of communion with one another, God, and all creation.

Chapter 9

How Do I Protect Myself?

He was the chief of police, entrusted with the safety of a city's citizens. Everyone was stunned when he shot his wife in a crowded parking lot, then turned the gun on himself. As local newspaper and television reporters investigated the incident, they discovered a long history of domestic violence in this family. The facts were especially disturbing because the abuser was a prominent police officer, but the story could have come from a family anywhere in the world. It is deeply troubling but nonetheless true that for many women and children, the most dangerous place is their own home. They frequently experience the greatest harm from those they count on to love and protect them. And contrary to common belief, domestic violence is not limited to any age, race, religion, education, occupation, or socioeconomic level.[1]

Secrets happen in families. Forgiving requires that we deal honestly with the dark undercurrents of family life, with the cruelty of bad homes. When we see only the good in those closest to us, we leave ourselves open to abuse and vengeance. We can forgive others and at the same time take the steps necessary to ensure our own safety.

The question *Will I be hurt again?* arises not only in situations of violence and abuse but in the daily push-and-pull of family life. Many people undertake the process of forgiving only when assured that it will not make them vulnerable to the offending person. They want no part of a forgiveness that exposes them to ongoing hurt. We must therefore understand what the gospel asks of us. It does not require us to remain in situations of danger or to put up with ongoing hurt. Protecting ourselves from harm is our right and duty.

Jesus himself practiced the advice he gave his disciples: "See, I am sending you out like sheep into the midst of wolves; so be wise as serpents and innocent as doves" (Matt. 10:16). Fully aware of the sin and evil in the world, Jesus did not walk into the traps of others. After he cleansed the Temple of the money changers, he knew his life was in danger and delayed going to Jerusalem until ready.

For Jesus, forgiveness is no rerun of the old order. It creates the conditions necessary for a fresh start. Being his disciples does not mean exposing ourselves again and again to the same old hurts. It does mean caring enough about relationships to take steps to live them differently.

Mistaken ideas about the requirements of forgiveness prevent us from being "wise as serpents." Read the following list of false beliefs that many people hold. Which of them endanger your safety or prevent you from forgiving?

MYTHS ABOUT FORGIVENESS

1. Forgiveness requires me to stay in an abusive or violent relationship. Absolutely not. In situations of violence and abuse, safety must be the primary concern. If you or someone you know is in such a relationship, get professional help. Domestic violence is a complex and potentially dangerous situation; those with the experience and skill to respond appropriately should handle it. The best course of action for both the battered and the batterer is referral to a professional counselor, because each needs specialized help. Become acquainted with sources of help in your area, such as domestic violence hotlines, emergency shelters for the battered, and treatment programs for those who batter. These resources can provide safety and wisdom for the battered and accountability and sanctions for an assaultive spouse.

Too often women seeking help with domestic abuse receive admonitions to forgive, return to their husbands, and make their marriages work. We should not press persons in these situations to forgive. A spouse may already blame herself for the violence or abuse: "It was my fault; I could tell when he was going to go into a rage. I just said something that set him off." If a woman's religious tradition tells her that a good wife submits to her husband; that patience, obedience, and gentleness are womanly virtues; that suffering is to be endured; and that nothing justifies leaving a marriage, then she needs sound spiritual counseling. Emphasis on keeping a family together at all costs ignores the fact that over time, without intervention, abusive behavior tends to increase in frequency and severity.

> *Some family members are so dangerous that we have to isolate and protect ourselves from them, at least for a time.*

Fear of being hurt again is well-founded when the offense is intentional and repeated and the offender shows no repentance. Forgiveness then becomes a way for the abused person to heal and get internally free, but reconciliation is not possible. Victims of family abuse may find that they cannot have a relationship with the abuser again, although, after healing work, they no longer hate the abuser. Forgiveness may even give some the courage to leave a destructive relationship. Some family members are so dangerous, and the harm they cause so severe, that the abused persons have to isolate and protect themselves from the offender, at least for a time.

Recall that forgiving starts with an honest look at how we have been hurt. It asks us to recognize the source of our pain. For a relationship to continue, the one forgiven must learn from past mistakes and thoroughly renounce them. Since false promises of such repentance are part of the cycle of domestic abuse, persons in these relationships may need help to avoid succumbing to them.

2. *Forgiving is the same as being nice.* Women are especially apt to confuse forgiveness with being nice. Being nice is not a Christian virtue. It is simply a socially acceptable way of dealing with situations, one that women have been taught to observe since they were little girls. And it can put them at risk of physical and emotional harm.

Forgiveness does not preclude self-defense, protecting ourselves from harm, or saying no when a boundary has been threatened. It does not prevent us from learning to stay safe around dangerous family members. Nor does it mean giving up claims to justice and compensation.

An ancient tale illustrates this truth. Long ago there was a village with a saint living nearby. As he walked among the hills one day, the saint encountered a snake lying in the grass. Fangs bared, the snake lunged at the holy man as though it would bite him. But when the saint smiled, the snake was stopped by his kindness. The saint suggested that the rattler quit biting the children of the village. He pointed out that the snake would be better liked and cause less harm.

The snake agreed to follow the holy man's suggestion because he sensed his power. A week passed. When the saint went walking again, he found the snake lying on the ground, surrounded by blood. The snake berated the saint for the advice that had almost killed him: "Look what happened to me when I took your advice. I am a bloody mess. Look what happened to me when I tried to be nice and not bite, and now everyone is trying to hurt me."

The saint replied, "I never told you not to hiss."[2]

To hiss is to set limits and take steps to protect ourselves when necessary. It is to insist that family members get treatment for addiction and serious mental illness. It recognizes that, as much as we may want to deny it, abusers, rapists, murderers, and thieves all belong to somebody's family. When that family is our own, we will neither help the person nor ourselves if we settle for being nice. Forgiving should not turn us into doormats.

Unfortunately some who are close to us, even in our own families, act like enemies toward us. In these situations, forgiving calls for something much more exacting than being nice. We must struggle again and again with dilemmas: What does it mean to love such enemies? How do we keep our anger toward them from petrifying into hatred and a desire for their destruction?

3. *Forgiveness means forgetting the offense.* You may think you have forgotten the way your sister-in-law criticized your parenting skills. Then you see her at the next family gathering and try to avoid talking to her. Forgiveness is not a form of amnesia.

In fact, remembering is important to our safety. If we forget, the pattern may repeat itself. A woman describes how her recent birthday started out to be a happy day. Then her daughter ripped into her, laying out all her faults. Now she fears talking to her daughter again. "I don't think I can take another attack like that. Am I really that miserable a mother?" She will not likely forget the event, nor will pretending that she has forgotten help her. Another woman sums up her view of the problem: "Family burns you. You go back, and they burn you again." These women need strategies for preventing such hurts from recurring. What can they change about the situations or their own actions? If they simply forget, they will walk right into the same pain again.

Forgiveness brings about a change of seasons. We do not completely forget the interval of pain, but we do not live forever in its frigid climate. We let go of anger and bitterness but maintain awareness that what was done to us was wrong. After a hurt, attitudes of caution will persist until trust has been rebuilt. As events play out over time, we discover whether or not our trust is well-founded.

> *Forgiveness brings about a change of seasons. We do not completely forget the pain, but we do not live forever in its frigid climate.*

4. *My world will be the same as before the hurt.* When a parent, spouse, or other family member hurts us, the incident shatters our bedrock assumptions about life. Such wounding brings us up against the meaning of suffering and evil. It shakes our trust, our belief in justice, our opinion of ourselves, our faith in the goodness of people, and our conviction that God will protect us against harm. It destroys the idealized images of marriage and family we once cherished. While going through a divorce, a man laments: "How

can I believe in anything anymore if I can't trust this woman I lived so close to for twenty years? I've lost all faith in myself. Why didn't I notice what was going on?"

At such times we can truly pray with the psalmist:

Save me, O God,
      for the waters have come up to my neck.
I sink in deep mire,
      where there is no foothold;
I have come into deep waters,
      and the flood sweeps over me. (Psalm 69:1-2)

This is one reason why "I forgive" is not a phrase tossed out in passing. It reaches into all areas of our lives. We learn that it is possible to feel both love and anger toward the same person, a difficult concept for children but necessary for adults. We develop a new understanding of family, one that may have to incorporate infidelity, incest, theft, and lies. We relinquish attempts to understand fully the *why* of suffering, the desire to get to the bottom of the pain another has caused us.

Ultimately the answer to the question *Will I be hurt again?* is yes. At bottom, forgiveness offers love to someone who has betrayed that love in small or large ways. This healing process cannot fail to have a profound impact on us. Inevitably it leads to new beliefs about ourselves and relationships. We now know what it is to take a chance on loving others, but we can also make better choices about whether a particular gamble is one we should take. Forgiving reveals more fully our own limits and sinfulness and those of other family members. The English essayist C. S. Lewis remarks in his book *The Four Loves* that if we choose to love at all, we become vulnerable: "Love anything, and your heart will certainly be wrung and possibly be broken." The only way to prevent vulnerability, he says, is to refuse to love at all. But a heart locked up safely in this way will change nonetheless: "It will not be broken; it will become unbreakable, impenetrable, irredeemable."[3]

Eventually we integrate the recurrence of hurt into our worldview. We know it will happen again, but the experience no longer shatters our world. Forgiving takes us into what the gospel describes as a Christlike maturity. Jesus knew the evil in the world but did not let it deflect him from love and action. He experienced betrayal but continued to trust; his commitment to his mission took him to the Cross. The wounds he endured were still present after the Resurrection, visible in his hands and feet but transformed. Jesus promises that our own resurrections, including those experienced in family life, will bring this same kind of healing. His promise undergirds our prayer as we attempt to honor both a concern for safety and the call to forgiveness.

Merciful God,
Look with compassion on my plight. The person who hurt me,
whose violence I fear, is not a stranger on the street but some-
one close to me, a member of my own family.

My pain and confusion are deep and, at times, over-
whelming. My faith falters like a tree shaken by strong wind.
Where are you, my God?

I believe you are with me. You understand my fear and
doubt. You walk with me as I seek healing and peace. You are
the companion on whom I can rely, a faithful friend in whose
presence I can feel safe again.

Show me how to see my situation in new ways. Give me
the grace to discern wisely and the courage to do what I must.
Do not let this betrayal scar my heart forever; help me remain
open to love.

Amen.

Chapter 10

Fostering Family Forgiveness

A modern fable called *It's Mine!* depicts the beauty of being at peace with those close to us. In the middle of Rainbow Pond is a small island. On it live three frogs named Milton, Rupert, and Lydia. From daybreak to sunset the frogs quarrel and quibble. Each screams to the others to get out of the water, leave the island, or stop jumping at the butterflies. "It's mine," they shout about each of these wonders of their island home.

Then the skies darken and thunder rumbles. A violent storm sweeps through, and the island grows smaller and smaller, swept away by the rising waters. The frogs are left clinging to a single rock. Soaked and terrified, they suddenly realize that they each have the same hopes and fears; they feel better now that they are together. They make peace with one another.

At last the rains stop and the flood subsides. Together the frogs swim around the island and leap to catch the butterflies. They are happier than they have ever been.

> "Isn't it peaceful," said Milton.
> "And isn't it beautiful," said Rupert.
> "And do you know what else?" said Lydia.
> "No, what?" the others asked.
> "It's ours!" she said.[1]

Like the characters in this fable, we have moments when we realize what a gift it is to be part of a family. Survivors with only one lifeboat, we come together and find that we have been taking our grievances far too seriously.

> *What we do in ordinary times to strengthen family ties makes it easier to move through the hurtful events that inevitably occur.*

We need not wait for tragedy to strike to learn this lesson. Just as a car is less likely to break down at critical times if regularly maintained, so what we do in ordinary times to strengthen family ties makes it easier to move through the hurtful events that inevitably occur. This ongoing maintenance also teaches our children forgiveness as a way of life. A strong family gives them a circle of people with whom they can identify, values and traditions they can make their own, and a web of support they can depend on when they need it. There are several ways to create a climate in which forgiveness thrives.

MAXIMIZE THE POSITIVE

Taking steps to build love and trust creates the conditions of forgiveness and reconciliation. Small and large acts of love tell individuals that family members care for them and have their happiness at heart. They learn to see love as a quality that increases as it is shared. The goal is to become a family that expresses appreciation, affirms the good qualities in one another, and celebrates special occasions. Just as an injury heals faster if we are in good overall health, so broken bonds mend more easily if a family has already worked to strengthen them.

Building family connections sometimes means going against cultural patterns of blame. For example, society tends to hold mothers responsible for most of what goes wrong in their children's lives. This leads to an unexamined habit of criticizing a mother for anything less than perfect parenting. Such relentless scrutiny especially harms mother/daughter relationships. Rejecting this societal pattern opens the way for mothers and daughters to develop a new appreciation for each other.

John Gottman, a professor at the University of Washington, has spent decades trying to determine why marriages succeed or fail. He observed that couples in lasting marriages experience five times as many positive exchanges as negative ones. By positive exchanges, he means simple actions like thanking a spouse for filling the gas tank, bringing home flowers from time to time, telling our mate we like what he or she is wearing, kissing each other before rushing off to work. When positive energy flows, a marriage can much more readily handle negative events like anger and hurt.[2]

The same is true of families. When we find simple ways to increase the positive energy throughout the family system, we can more easily survive the inevitable disappointments and conflicts. Like a fortified cable that can bear the weight of a heavier load, the relationship that has been strengthened over time more readily withstands the normal hurts. A history of love and respect enables family members to look beyond painful words or actions. A previous record of trust provides reason to risk trusting again.

Positive family patterns sow hope, like the acorn seeds in Jean Giono's story *The Man Who Planted Trees*. Giono recounts how he once visited a barren region in Provence, France, where only wild lavender grew. Everything in the area lay in ruins, and Giono found few signs of life. He spent the night in a village where rivalries and grievances infected every exchange. But there he met a shepherd who spent his days quietly planting hundreds of acorns in the desolate land.

Eventually Giono moved on, forgetting about the shepherd and his acorns. But when he returned to the region a decade later, he was amazed to see what these simple acorns had brought about. A carpet of oak trees now covered the mountaintops. Not only that, but the planting had set off a chain reaction. Water flowed once more in the dry streams. With the water came meadows, gardens, flowers, and willows. Even the air had changed. What had been a harsh wind from the nearby mountains now was filled with pleasant scents. A transformation had gradually taken place. Hope had returned. The village was now a place where people thrived.[3]

LEARN TO APPRECIATE DIFFERENCES

My husband, Tom, and I both come from large families. He had eight brothers and sisters, and I had seven. Add spouses, nieces, nephews, grandparents, aunts, uncles, and cousins, and you have two very complicated clans. Relating to this colorful tribe over the years has taught me just how rich, and at the same time demanding, family life can be.

Families are complex systems. People we would never choose as close associates become, by reason of birth, forever a part of our intimate network. To complicate matters further, we are brought into association with in-laws because someone else in the family loves them. Sometimes we like these people, and great relationships result. But amid this gathering of people, we sometimes find those with whom we differ sharply as well as those we dislike, maybe even intensely.

How can we all get along? The way we view differences is key. Do we translate differences into right and wrong? Or can we learn to view them as enrichment and possibly even a graced stimulus to our own expansion? A good exercise is to pause once in a while and name the ways that sometimes-irksome differences may also be gifts to us and our family. Can we learn to love others as they are?

When patterns of behavior do not harm an individual or other family members—as does chronic alcohol or drug abuse, violence, or sexual abuse—acceptance becomes the key to peace. A grandmother who disagreed with many things about the lifestyles of her grandchildren commented, "But I think I owe it to them to let them live their own lives without my interference, the way I want to be allowed to live my own life."

PRACTICE FORGIVENESS SKILLS DAILY

Part of the problem with forgiving is that no one ever taught us how. Like swimming or playing the piano, forgiveness improves with practice. If we rehearse the art of forgiving in small matters, we will find it easier to deal with the big ones.

It is wonderful to hear a parent say to a child: "I'm sorry I screamed at you when you dropped that dish. Mistakes happen, and that was not a good way for me to react. I'll try not to do it again." From this interchange a child learns how to acknowledge one's failure and ask for forgiveness. Another family shared how, after a bad weekend, they each admitted that they had been crabby and out of sorts. They acknowledged that they had taken their bottled-up anger out on one another. Then they talked about what they were going to do with that anger instead. One would write in her journal. Another would list all the things she was angry about and see what she could do about them. The mother promised she would talk with a friend about what was bothering her.

How different these lessons are from those we might have learned growing up. Deeply implanted in us may be reactions like these: Stomp out of the room when you are hurt. Clam up and sulk. Try to get others on your side. Rehearse all their faults over and over in your mind. All these reactions likely belong to our repertoire for handling hurts, but gradually we can replace them with more constructive approaches.

SET ASIDE IDEALIZED FAMILY IMAGES

Growing up, I often longed to belong to a more peaceful family than the one I lived with. But over the years I have learned that those perfect sitcom families exist only on TV. Our longing to be like them is part of an understandable hunger for release from all the suffering and limitations of this life.

Perhaps you have seen paintings by Norman Rockwell, whose depictions of family life appeared for many years on the cover of *The Saturday Evening Post*. His pictures portrayed idealized images of family life. For example, one painting shows a smiling family gathered around a Thanksgiving table spread with festive food. No frowns or signs of tension mar the occasion. All the family members, including the children, appear to be engaged in lively conversation. Grandpa stands behind Grandma as she holds a huge platter with a perfectly roasted turkey. She appears refreshed and relaxed, in spite of having just pulled together a major meal. Whether or not you have seen a Rockwell painting, you may hold in your mind a similar image of what family should be. We all long for peace and family togetherness.

Life in most families bears faint resemblance to these paintings. On holidays things seem to be going well; then suddenly an argument arises, and a tense silence falls over the group. When I tell my counseling clients that all families struggle, they seem surprised. They think they are the exception, more troubled and less well put together than all other families on the planet. They wonder how their little clan could be so broken when other families seem so happy. The truth is, families are not what they appear to be to outsiders. Norman Rockwell's family lineage was filled with problems. For years his parents refused to speak to him. He knew the pain of depression and addiction, the sorrow of not being loved well by those who are supposed to love you most. He painted scenes that represented not his experience but his hopes.[4]

> *Life in most families bears little resemblance to Norman Rockwell paintings.*

Hurts occur in every family; we are not yet redeemed. In making forgiveness such an essential part of his message about loving relationships, Jesus was a realist. His community of friends is surprisingly similar to our own families. There are sinners and bunglers. Misunderstandings abound. His disciples harm one another, either intentionally or without realizing it. And Jesus' own family has the same characteristics. His mother does not fully understand what he is about. People tell her that her son is crazy and a troublemaker. We see her trying to make sense of it right up to the end.

Family experiences are a mixture of beauty and tragedy. When we grasp this truth, we understand why forgiveness constitutes such an essential part of family life. We truly do have to forgive again and again. Jesus' words match our experience of living close to others: "And if the same person sins against you seven times a day, and turns back to you seven times and says, 'I repent,' you must forgive" (Luke 17:4). To be able to forgive so many times, we need to take our family concerns often to God in prayer. As we embrace these imperfect, struggling people before God, our prayer may go something like the following:

Dear God,
You are father and mother, even sister and brother, to us, and much more than any of these, yet somehow revealed in all our relationships. I bring before you my family with all its joy and pain.

What would I be without my family? Thank you for all it has given me. I praise you for the fun of birthday parties and picnics, softball and card games, bandaged knees and mended hearts.

At times we are a pretty broken bunch, struggling to stick together. Bless us, and help us reach out to one another in healing and hope.

Wrap our family in your tender care, and show us your face in one another, especially our most hurting members. When our hearts become hardened, soften them, lest anger and hatred make a permanent home with us.

You are our refuge through all ages. Heal the wounds we have inherited from past generations, and protect our future members from bitter legacies. Let our family life grace not only each member but the universe as well.

Amen.

Notes

CHAPTER 1: WHAT IS FORGIVENESS?

1. Wendy M. Wright, *Seasons of a Family's Life: Cultivating the Contemplative Spirit at Home* (San Francisco: Jossey-Bass, 2003), 113–14.

CHAPTER 2: WHY SHOULD I FORGIVE?

1. Victor Hugo, *Les Misérables*, trans. Charles E. Wilbour (New York: Simon & Schuster, 1964), 29–30.

2. For a summary of research on forgiveness and health, see Michael E. McCullough, Kenneth I. Pargament, and Carl E. Thoresen, eds., *Forgiveness: Theory, Research, and Practice* (New York: The Guilford Press, 2000), 91–110 and 254–80.

CHAPTER 3: REFUSING TO GET EVEN

1. The Rutba story comes from the account by Doug Hostetter, Peace Pastor, Evanston Mennonite Church, and Senior Middle East Correspondent, American Friends Service Committee. It was sent by e-mail to supporters of the Christian Peacemaker Teams, as well as to representatives of the media, on March 30, 2003.

Chapter 4: Dealing with Anger

1. To learn more about anger, see Carol Tavris, *Anger: The Misunderstood Emotion*, rev. ed. (New York: Touchstone Books, 1989); Kathleen R. Fischer, *Transforming Fire: Women Using Anger Creatively* (Mahwah, NJ: Paulist Press, 1999); and Carroll Saussy, *The Gift of Anger: A Call to Faithful Action* (Louisville, KY.: Westminster John Knox Press, 1995).

2. Judith Wallerstein, Julia Lewis, and Sandra Blakeslee, *The Unexpected Legacy of Divorce: A 25 Year Landmark Study* (New York: Hyperion, 2000), 5–6.

Chapter 5: Who Do I Really Need to Forgive?

1. The man's comment on his remorse is from Lin Bauer et al., "Exploring Self-Forgiveness," *Journal of Religion and Health* 31 (1992): 154.

2. Mary Jo Meadow explains these elements of the Buddhist prayer of loving-kindness in a clear and helpful way in *Gentling the Heart: Buddhist Loving-Kindness Practice for Christians* (New York: Crossroad Publishing Company, 1994), 61–63 and 71–75.

Chapter 6: Changing Habits of the Heart

1. The Zen story of the monks and the woman is from Anthony de Mello, *The Song of the Bird*, 2nd ed. (Anand, India: Gujarat Sahitya Prakash, 1982), 138–39.

2. Patricia Raybon, *My First White Friend: Confessions on Race, Love, and Forgiveness* (New York: Penguin Books, 1996), 123–26.

3. Terry D. Hargrave, *Families and Forgiveness: Healing Wounds in the Intergenerational Family* (New York: Brunner/Mazel Publishers, 1994), 17–19.

CHAPTER 7: IT OFTEN HAPPENS BY INCHES

1. The tale of the dove and the coal-mouse is from Joseph Jaworski, *Synchronicity: The Inner Path of Leadership*, ed. Betty Sue Flowers (San Francisco: Berrett-Koehler Publishers, 1998), 197.

2. James Carroll, *An American Requiem: God, My Father, and the War That Came Between Us* (Boston: Houghton Mifflin Company, 1996), 262.

CHAPTER 9: HOW DO I PROTECT MYSELF?

1. The opening story is that of the chief of police of Tacoma, Washington, and his wife. See Maureen O'Hagan and Cheryl Phillips, "When a Wife's Abuser Is a Cop, Who Can Help?" *The Seattle Times*, May 9, 2003, A1 and A19. Helpful discussions of domestic violence can be found in Carol J. Adams and Marie M. Fortune, eds., *Violence against Women and Children: A Christian Theological Sourcebook* (New York: Continuum International Publishing Company, 1995); Pamela Cooper-White, *The Cry of Tamar: Violence against Women and the Church's Response* (Minneapolis: Fortress Press, 2003); and Neil Jacobson and John Gottman, *When Men Batter Women: New Insights into Ending Abusive Relationships* (New York: Simon & Schuster, 1998). While the battering of husbands does occur, it happens less frequently than violence against women. The guidelines

described in these books apply to all instances of spouse battering.

2. The story of the snake is told by Fred Luskin, *Forgive for Good: A Proven Prescription for Health and Happiness* (New York: HarperCollins Publishers, 2003), 192.

3. C. S. Lewis, *The Four Loves* (London: Fontana Books, 1963), 111.

Chapter 10: Fostering Family Forgiveness

1. Leo Lionni, *It's Mine!* (New York: Alfred A. Knopf, 1986), 26.

2. John Gottman with Nan Silver, *Why Marriages Succeed or Fail . . . And How You Can Make Yours Last* (New York: Fireside, 1995), 29 and 181–84.

3. Jean Giono, *The Man Who Planted Trees* (White River Junction, VT: Chelsea Green Publishing Company, 1985).

4. An account of Rockwell's struggles can be found in Laura Claridge, *Norman Rockwell: A Life* (New York: Random House, 2001), 218–21 and 352–55.

Selected Bibliography

Augsburger, David W. *Helping People Forgive*. Louisville, KY: Westminster John Knox Press, 1996.

Enright, Robert D. *Forgiveness Is a Choice: A Step-by-Step Process for Resolving Anger and Restoring Hope*. Washington, DC: American Psychological Association, 2001.

Enright, Robert D., and Joanna North, eds. *Exploring Forgiveness*. Madison, WI: The University of Wisconsin Press, 1998.

Govier, Trudy. *Forgiveness and Revenge*. New York: Routledge, 2002.

Haber, Joram Graf. *Forgiveness*. Savage, MD: Rowman & Littlefield Publishers, 1991.

Hargrave, Terry D. *Families and Forgiveness: Healing Wounds in the Intergenerational Family*. New York: Brunner/Mazel Publishers, 1994.

Jones, L. Gregory. *Embodying Forgiveness: A Theological Analysis*. Grand Rapids, MI: William B. Eerdmans Publishing Company, 1995.

Luskin, Fred. *Forgive for Good: A Proven Prescription for Health and Happiness*. New York: HarperCollins Publishers, 2003.

McCullough, Michael E., Kenneth I. Pargament, and Carl E. Thoresen, eds. *Forgiveness: Theory, Research, and Practice*. New York: Guilford Press, 2000.

Müller-Fahrenholz, Geiko. *The Art of Forgiveness: Theological Reflections on Healing and Reconciliation.* Geneva: World Council of Churches, 1997.

Murphy, Jeffrie G., and Jean Hampton. *Forgiveness and Mercy.* Cambridge: Cambridge University Press, 1988.

Volf, Miroslav. *Exclusion and Embrace: A Theological Exploration of Identity, Otherness, and Reconciliation.* Nashville, TN: Abingdon Press, 1996.

Walsh, Froma, ed. *Spiritual Resources in Family Therapy.* New York: Guilford Press, 1999.

Wright, Wendy M. *Seasons of a Family's Life: Cultivating the Contemplative Spirit at Home.* San Francisco: Jossey-Bass, 2003.

Suggested Reading

Brizee, Robert. *Eight Paths to Forgiveness*. St. Louis, MO: Chalice Press, 1998.

Clendenen, Avis, and Troy Martin, eds. *Forgiveness: Finding Freedom through Reconciliation*. New York: Crossroad Publishing Company, 2002.

Klug, Lyn, ed. *A Forgiving Heart: Prayers for Blessing and Reconciliation*. Minneapolis: Augsburg Fortress Publishers, 2003.

Linn, Dennis, Sheila Fabricant Linn, and Matthew Linn. *Don't Forgive Too Soon: Extending the Two Hands That Heal*. Mahwah, NJ: Paulist, 1997.

Meninger, William A. *The Process of Forgiveness*. New York: Continuum Publishing Group, 1997.

Simon, Sidney B., and Suzanne Simon. *Forgiveness: How to Make Peace with Your Past and Get on with Your Life*. New York: Warner Books, 1990.

Smedes, Lewis B. *The Art of Forgiving: When You Need to Forgive and Don't Know How*. New York: Ballantine, 1997.

Tutu, Desmond. *No Future without Forgiveness*. New York: Doubleday, 1999.

Weaver, Andrew J., and Monica Furlong, eds., *Reflections on Forgiveness and Spiritual Growth*. Nashville, TN: Abingdon Press, 2000.

Wuellner, Flora Slosson. *Forgiveness, the Passionate Journey: Nine Steps of Forgiving through Jesus' Beatitudes.* Nashville, TN: Upper Room Books, 2001.

About the Author

KATHLEEN FISCHER works as a psychotherapist and spiritual director in Seattle. Dr. Fischer has worked with families in various settings for the past twenty years. She has also taught in several ministry training programs where the topic of family forgiveness comprised part of the training: Boston College, Notre Dame, and Seattle University. She received a PhD from the Graduate Theological Union, Berkeley, California; a Master of Theology from Marquette University, Milwaukee, Wisconsin; and a Master of Social Work from the University of Washington, Seattle.

Dr. Fischer is the author of several books—*Winter Grace: Spirituality and Aging; Transforming Fire: Women Using Anger Creatively; Autumn Gospel: Women in the Second Half of Life; Women at the Well: Feminist Perspectives on Spiritual Direction; The Inner Rainbow: The Imagination in Christian Life;* and *Imaging Life after Death: Love That Moves the Sun and Stars.* She has written numerous articles on spirituality and the intersection of spirituality and psychology and coauthored several other books with her husband, Thomas Hart.

Don't miss these other titles from Upper Room Books

Forgiveness, the Passionate Journey
Nine Steps of Forgiving through Jesus' Beatitudes
by Flora Slosson Wuellner

"Forgiveness is a perilous and volatile subject because it is so deeply intertwined with our communal and individual wounds," says Flora Wuellner. In this book Wuellner explores how Jesus' Beatitudes promise release from these wounds. Whether you have deep wounds or are worn down by a multitude of seemingly small grievances, Wuellner's insights into the Beatitudes will introduce you to the renewed and healed life Jesus offers there. Each chapter includes a guided meditation to help bring the truth of Jesus' words into your life.

ISBN 0-8358-0945-5 • 160 pages

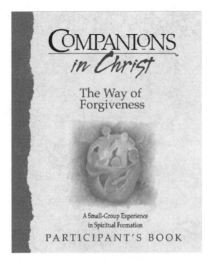

**Companions in Christ:
The Way of
Forgiveness**
Participant's Book
by Marjorie Thompson

This eight-week study
for individuals or small
groups challenges
participants to live a
forgiven and forgiving
life in response to
God's call.

Weekly themes include
  • living in God's blessing
  • releasing shame and guilt
  • facing our anger
  • transforming anger
  • receiving God's forgiveness
  • forgiving others
  • seeking reconciliation
  • becoming the beloved community
ISBN 0-8358-0980-3 • 120 pages

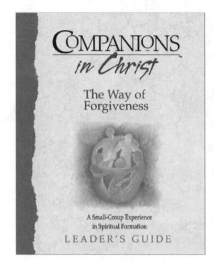

Companions in Christ:
The Way of
Forgiveness
Leader's Guide
by Stephen Bryant and
Marjorie Thompson

The Leader's Guide
offers complete con-
tent for leading each
weekly small-group
session, practical tips
for leading formational
groups, an easy-to-follow format, and a rich variety of
experiences for participants.
ISBN 0-8358-0981-1 • 96 pages